DAVID B

SINGLE
FOR A
SEASON

HOW TO BE SINGLE AND HAPPY
A GUIDE FOR CHRISTIAN SINGLES

Single for a Season: How to Be Single and Happy—A Guide for Christian Singles

David Brühlmann

Published by Swissthrive: www.swissthrive.com

ISBN 978-3-9525423-0-9

To single people living around the world who dream of living life to the fullest—you pushed me to write my first book. It's my honor to help you keep your dream alive. You have within you all the resources necessary to make this time one of the most exciting, meaningful seasons of your life.

CONTENTS

INTRODUCTION

It happened on a day like any other. I was having dinner with friends at a restaurant. We'd just ordered appetizers when a beautiful woman approached our group, walking with an air of quiet confidence. I couldn't help staring at her cascading dark hair and round brown eyes. She was beautiful.

"Hi, Jessica. How are you?" she said to one of my friends. "Thanks for inviting me." Her voice was warm and friendly.

When we sat down for dinner, I made sure to sit next to her and greatly enjoyed speaking with her and listening to her conversations with others. As we ate our meals, I thought, "She's funny, has a fabulous sense of style, is well-educated, and she follows Jesus!" These were all attributes I was looking for in a life partner. By the end of the evening, I believed my sad existence as a single was about to end. I was so sure she liked me, too; I announced to friends, "I've met my dream wife. She's mind-blowing!" I walked around singing, "Love is in the air, everywhere I look around ... "

Not wanting to appear too eager, I waited a bit before texting her to ask her out for a date. I was shocked when she responded, "No thank you. I don't date strangers."

I stared at her message with utter confusion and then texted back, "We're not strangers; we had dinner together," but she refused to reconsider.

I was sure she'd change her mind if she got to know me better, so, over the next few weeks, I texted her a few times and sent her hand-crafted cards. When we happened to run into each other one evening, I was very happy to see her again and invited her to join me at an upcoming BBQ with friends. She politely—but firmly—turned me down and indicated she had no interest in having a relationship with me.

I was crushed. Once again, a woman I was in love with chose not to become my life partner. I would have to continue my life as a single person, waiting to find the right woman to spend my life with. I believed I had been single for far too long—much longer than I had planned. I was confused and asked myself many painful questions: "Why didn't she like me? Is something wrong with me? Why am I single while many of my friends have found their soulmates? Is there anything I can do to find mine? Am I missing out? What should I do while I'm waiting? What is God's purpose for me?"

I searched for answers, talked to my pastor and friends, and read books on the subject. And then I found this passage in the Bible:

To everything there is a season, and a time to every purpose under the heaven.

—ECCLESIASTES 3:1

This gave me hope because it means that seasons are part of God's nature and part of our lives, too. We don't need to spend our lives waiting for the season of marriage because a different season has already arrived. "To everything there is a season" means there is a season to be single, too, and at this time in our lives, our "purpose under the heaven" is to be single. I also discovered that God has a definite purpose for us in our single season: He wants us to thrive.

As singles, we have a choice: we can either await relief from our unmarried lives, or we can find our God-given unique purpose in this season of being single. I chose the latter. Before my attitude adjustment, I was upset and dissatisfied. Afterward, I felt peaceful and content. Why? I realized that my only viable option was living my single life now instead of simply passing the time, waiting for my married life to begin.

> *I perceived that there is nothing better for them than to be joyful and to do good as long as they live.*
>
> **—ECCLESIASTES 3:12**

Although I am still looking forward to the day when I find my soulmate, I have become a fulfilled single. While it is not my preference to be single, I have learned to live in this space of tension and to find meaning, joy, and God's love. I certainly have not found the answers to all of my confusing questions. Rather, I have realized I don't need all of the answers to thrive.

Through my many years of work in various church ministries, I have spent much time with other Christian singles, discussing the difficulties of the single season and brainstorming ways to deal with them. In preparation for writing this book, I contacted single men and women from around the globe to get their unique perspectives on these issues. Then I read blogs, watched videos, studied the Bible, and looked at research articles to find out even more.

My singleness enabled me to invest in my education, learn many foreign languages, and develop a successful corporate career. Recently, I left a high-paying managerial position in research and development and relocated from Switzerland to Cambodia. Thinking someone should do something to give young people access to excellent education in Cambodia, I realized it might as well be me.

I wrote *Single for a Season* because I want to help other singles like you thrive, too. And you know what? You can! Right now. Yes, you can thrive while being single. Through this book, you can join me on a journey of discovery where I chronicle my successes, failures, struggles, insights, faith, strength, and love.

In a nutshell, *Single for a Season* will help you do the following:

- Overcome the confusion, frustration, and loneliness of being single

- Heal wounds of past relationships and find confidence

- Become whole and thrive as a single person

- Find your purpose and make the most of your single season

- Realize you are not missing out so you can wait in peace

- Make space in your life for a future relationship

I have discovered great joy, purpose, and meaning in my life while being single, which I would like to share with you. Because all of us are different and have different questions and goals, I will not try to give you definite answers, but instead will tell you about my experiences. I have also invited several singles from all over the world to describe their experiences as singles, too, and have included their stories in each chapter of the book.

Through this book, I pray that God will reveal to you your unique purpose in this season of singleness. At the end of Creation, God looked at His work and saw that it was excellent. This was not a coincidence because everything God does has a purpose. This applies to your life as well, even if sometimes you may not feel this is the case. You have a purpose in this beautiful single season.

He has made everything beautiful in its time.

—ECCLESIASTES 3:11

When you read *Single for a Season,* I hope God will give you a new perspective. I invite you to prepare your heart for this journey by praying to Him that He helps you lay aside your frustrations, confusion, and hurts so that He may speak to you in a new and fresh way. You will be astonished at how your Father in Heaven will use this book to help you learn to thrive while single.

Let's get started!

CHAPTER 1

MOVING FROM CONFUSION TO CLARITY

There is nothing wrong with you. It's just not your time yet. Let go of the idea that being single means something is wrong with you. The only thing that being single means … is that you're single.

—MANDY HALE, AUTHOR AND SPEAKER

STORY OF A SINGLE

I feel odd being single in my forties. I'm not clear on why I'm still single and if I want to remain single. It wasn't my intention to stay single this long. And yet, I realized it has allowed me to devote more time and energy to running a home for orphaned and abandoned children in Southeast Asia. I couldn't have handled that amount of responsibility, commitment, and the countless crises if I were married with kids. But if you had told me when I was twenty-one, that I would still be single and celibate at this stage in my life, I probably would have looked for the exit ramp from Christian missions, and perhaps even for the exit ramp off of Christianity. I might have been tempted to think, "It's too high a price to pay. The grace of God is not going to be sufficient. I can't do it."

Sometimes I have clarity on why I'm single, and then other times, I might not have clarity but have learned a deeper sense of contentment. Singleness has not been this monolithic, unchanging experience. Instead, it has been seasonal, with warm summers and cold winters. I've had girlfriends whom I thought I would marry, but didn't. Through the years, I've cried more tears over women lost and hopes dashed than I ever thought possible. I was engaged when I was in my twenties. Years later, I was almost engaged again and thought I was going to get married, but it didn't happen.

I wonder if my attempts to end my singleness mean I am fighting against God. He's never spoken clearly to me about the reasons I remain single. I have doubts. Confusion sometimes invades and clouds my thoughts. I ask, "What's going on? Why is this happening to me?"

I have wondered if I am single because the Lord has been sovereignly protecting me from other women to preserve me for someone special who he plans to bring into my life. Or am I being picky, selfish, self-centered, and overly independent? It's likely a mixture of both. Hopefully, if I were to get married one day, I would realize that my difficult season of singleness was all worth it. My biggest lesson consisted of learning to be content and joyful despite my singleness.

At this stage in my life, I want a soul connection. If I were to get married, I want to share my life with someone in a deep, abiding friendship. If I feel I don't have enough in common with a woman, I have no enthusiasm to get married to her. I know I'll survive while being single. If I do end up getting married, it will enrich my life, but I won't see it as the solution to unhappiness because I'm not miserable *in singleness. I am open to marriage, but I'm not willing to settle for something less than God's revelation of marriage because I know too many unhappy married people.*

I've also decided not to place conditions on my service to God. In other words, I won't say, "God, I will only continue to do X, Y, and Z for You if You provide me with a wife." Doing so reverses the roles we should have. I must remember He is the Master and I am the slave—always.

But it's not easy. I do struggle with feelings of loneliness—at times, profound loneliness. I want to share my life with someone. Like when I'm on the summit of a mountain and looking at a beautiful sunset. I want to look over at someone special and say, "Isn't this awesome that we're sharing this moment so that we can talk about it ten years from now?" But there is no "someone special"—it's just me. However, I can't feel sorry for myself because of this. I must choose joy, thankfulness, and contentment.

I keep praying, "Lord, I would love for You to bring me a woman that uniquely complements me and shares the same vision that I do and is a wonderful friend."

—MATT, FORTY-FOUR YEARS OLD, UNITED STATES

One of my favorite animated movies is *Shrek*. Although I know the story is a cliché, the ogre's pursuit of the beautiful princess draws me in every single time. While watching it over and over again, I move from joy and laughter to excitement and tears and then back to joy again. It's a story about finding real love.

Finding my princess was my main goal for the better part of my life. Like Shrek, I did find my princess. But unlike Shrek, I was unable to win her heart. And this happened to me over and over again, with one princess after another. So now I am still single, which certainly was not my plan.

When I was thirty years old, I was alone once again after recently breaking up with someone, and my relationship status did not change from single to married as I approached thirty-five. For the next five years, I dated a few wonderful women, but as I neared forty, once again no princess was in sight. Today I'm still waiting to find my ideal marriage partner. I am a long-term single. Some may consider me a failure, someone with issues, or perhaps a person who is crazy and irresponsible. Friends and family members ask, "David, why are you still single?"

Being single is not my first choice since I don't have the gift of singleness. That is, I don't have the desire to spend my entire life single. I have prayed about it, reflected on it, and talked to many people about it, but one thing remains unchanged: my desire to get married. I grew up thinking I would meet my soulmate and get married one day. Since I have not found my princess yet, I was confused and wondered if something was wrong with me.

What about you? How long have you been waiting for your soulmate? Does it seem like an eternity? Do you feel like Matt, the single who shared his story at the beginning of this chapter, wondering if there is something wrong with you that is causing you to remain single? If so, you may have fallen victim to one of the myths told about being single.

MYTHS ABOUT BEING SINGLE

As singles, we believe many myths that leave us confused. For instance, we hear people say that singles are miserable because they lack an essential part: a soulmate. Have you noticed that when you hear a myth many times, you start to believe it? Let's review some common myths about the single life.

Myth #1: You Are Weird Because You Are Single

Let me tell you upfront, "You are normal!" Nothing is wrong with you because you are still single. I wish I heard this sentence more often when I was younger. If I had, it would not have taken me so long to understand the truth of this statement.

By saying, "I'm normal," I am not trying to justify my behavior and choices. I just mean that, like the many sublime singles I've met throughout my life, I am not weird just because I'm single. If you are still single, too, nothing is wrong with you either. I believe no relationship status defines whether you are weird, conventional, brilliant, or any other attribute you would like to add.

But I didn't always believe this. Thinking I was weird set me up for a destructive, self-critical, downward spiral, causing me to search for areas of my personality I needed to improve. Although it seemed like a good idea at the time, I was trying to fix myself for the wrong reasons. I was not trying to change to become a healthier person. Rather, I felt I had to change because of some perceived shortcoming in my character that caused me to remain single. It took me a long time to understand this wasn't good motivation for self-improvement.

We all have issues. I do, you do, and married people do, too. But please understand that nothing is wrong with us simply because we are single. The fact that you are reading this book means you want to learn how to become a better version of yourself. Kudos to you for your determination and your courage to do so. You're on the right track. Never forget you are normal. Actually, you are more than normal; you are unique, or even extraordinary. And that is the clarity I wish for you: that you know you are a great person. You have jaw-dropping gifts, impressive dreams, and a determination to be the best self you can be.

Never buy into the myth that you are weird just because you have not yet met your Princess or Prince Charming. It's a lie. You are awesome.

Myth #2: Singles Are Miserable

When I was at university, I thought older singles must live cheerless lives. How could they possibly be happy if they were not in a relationship? But Joanna Gaines, co-founder and co-owner of Magnolia Enterprises, wrote in *The Magnolia Story*, "I always thought that the 'thriving' would come when everything was perfect, and what I learned is that it's actually down in the mess that things get good." Like Ms. Gaines, I erroneously believed everything needed to be perfect for me to be happy. But then, like her, I realized that wasn't true. I learned just because I wanted to be in a romantic relationship did not mean I had to be unhappy while waiting for it; I could be happy anytime. Also, I figured out I did not have to be desperate, thinking I was missing the bandwagon as I was getting older and remained unmarried.

I found a better way to live. Rather than focusing on looking for "the one," I now focus on God, and I wait to see what the future has in store for me, confident that it will be the future I am meant to have. What is the source of my confidence? I know God has everything under control. My marital status no longer determines the state of my mind. If God is taking care of my situation, there is hope, even if I don't see it. This quote by self-help guru Dale Carnegie illustrates what focusing on God does for me: "Two men looked out from prison bars, one saw the mud, the other saw stars." When I focus on the stars instead of the mud, my life feels joyful. And because of this attitude adjustment, I now am more likely to meet singles who also are fulfilled and overflowing with joy and hope.

Myth #3: Being Married Is Better Than Being Single

What would your friend or pastor say if you asked him, "Is being married better than being single?" The apostle Paul would give you a definite answer: "No." He understood the benefits of his singleness: that it enabled him to live his dream. In the Roman empire 2,000 years ago, traveling throughout the Middle East and Southern Europe (Lebanon, Syria, Turkey, Cyprus, Greece, and Italy) was no easy endeavor, taking him many days or even weeks to reach his destinations. His journeys were dangerous and tiring, and he knew that he could not have accomplished his missions if he had a family at home who relied on him. Paul considered his relationship status as an outstanding privilege. He wrote:

> *Now, as a concession, not a command, I say this. I wish that all were as I am. But each has his gift from God, one of one kind and one of another. To the unmarried and the widows, I say that it is good for them to remain single, as I am.*
>
> **—1 CORINTHIANS 7:6-8**

Paul, the founder of the vast majority of the early churches, and the one who wrote two-thirds of the New Testament, was pro-single and encouraged singles to follow his examples.

Soak that in for a minute: being single is not inferior to being married, nor anything evil to avoid. Being single is good. Enjoy it.

Myth #4: Getting Married Is the Ultimate Goal

What happens if I never achieve my dream of getting married? How will I feel if I stay single my entire life? What is more important to me: getting married or doing God's will? If you asked Paul these questions, he would have said some of us are not supposed to be married. And that's the reason that some people decide to follow Paul's example and to embrace celibacy as a gift.

I don't think I have the gift of singleness or celibacy, and I told this to Jesus; I told Him I want to get married. But at the same time, I surrendered to him the right to do his will, which included the option of staying single and celibate. It was difficult for me to abandon my dream of getting married, and it took me a long time to get there, but that courageous decision has given me peace. I know no matter what happens, I will be fine. My desire to share my life with someone has not disappeared, but I am single for a season, and you may argue that I have the gift of celibacy for this season.

Although Paul promoted the choice of singleness, he thought marriage was good, too, and he felt that for many people, it was a better choice than staying single. He wrote:

But if they cannot exercise self-control, they should marry. For it is better to marry than to burn with passion.

—1 CORINTHIANS 7:9

Whether you marry or stay single, remember this: getting married is not the purpose of everyone's life, nor is a calling to have children. Paul accomplished God's mission as a single person with no children. I like to look at my singleness as a unique opportunity to serve the Lord. If I stay single another month, a year, or many years, I want to embrace it. And when—and if—my season as a single person comes to a close and a new relational season begins, I want to embrace that one, too. But I never want becoming married to be my sole purpose in life.

Myth #5: Singleness Is a Waiting Room for Marriage

Remember: God has a specific purpose for us in this season while we are single. Paul's teachings, once again, help us to gain the right perspective. Since he wrote that neither is better—being single or married—we know singleness is not a waiting room for married life, just as childhood is not a waiting room for adulthood. They are all high seasons to enjoy and cherish. If we spend our time as singles waiting for the chance to get married, we are doing nothing more than surviving, and that is far from what we should do: to thrive. You can choose to make your single season the best season of your life.

We tend to impatiently anticipate what is coming next because we think it will be better. When you stand in line to get into your favorite restaurant, you do it because you believe the dinner will be so much better than the long wait outside in the cold. I spent many years as a single person waiting, thinking that what was coming next—the married life—would be much better. I regret spending so much time waiting, not realizing that being single was an astounding season of my life. Try not to make the same mistake I did.

Someone once told me that she deliberately selected short-term projects while waiting for her soulmate to show up, and I realized that

I was guilty of doing the same thing. I was taking on a series of small, unimportant jobs so that when I found my princess and we decided to marry, I wouldn't have to consider whether our relationship would affect my dream job by causing me to move to another city for us to be together. I was biking through life with my handbrake on, never going too fast. That way, I could stop at any time. Was that an excellent way to live? Not at all. It kept me from having fulfilling experiences.

In my twenties, I wanted to have a girlfriend, but I didn't dwell on it too much. I cherished the multiple advantages I had while being single. For instance, I spent my third year of chemical engineering studies at a Canadian university. I didn't have to worry about leaving a girlfriend behind in Switzerland and so was able to fully enjoy meeting new people, discovering a country I had never seen, having more free time, and improving my piano skills.

A significant shift happened as I was nearing thirty years of age, and I realized I would not achieve my goal of being married by then. Instead of dwelling upon this as a failure, I learned there was much more to life than just waiting for my soulmate. I began to see singleness as a gift. The more I reflected on the matter, the more it dawned on me that I should find my special purpose in this single season and stop just waiting to get married. God wanted me to live my life to its fullest, and He wants that for you, too. There is no reason for us to grow desolate in our singleness; we can thrive.

Myth #6: If You Are Single, You Are Not Complete

Believing that single people are not whole individuals sets us up for disappointments and profound emotional hardships. I often dated women, thinking they'd be able to identify and fix what was missing in me. I was convinced I couldn't be a whole person without a partner in my life. Then I realized no spouse can complete me. And you won't find a soulmate who will fill all your voids, either. It is like a man buying an amazing sports car or a woman buying the most beautiful dress to make up for some deficit in their characters: it doesn't work.

As human beings—no matter if we are single, married, or divorced—we are never complete. We are flawed and none of us is perfect. The only way to find completeness is in God. As Paul wrote:

> *So you also are complete through your union with Christ.*
>
> **—COLOSSIANS 2:10 (NLT)**

You do not need a relationship with another person to be a whole person yourself. To quote television host and motivational speaker Mel Robbins, "No other person can complete you. You are not a puzzle with a missing piece." If you let Jesus fill you, He will make you complete now, in your single season. And—as a bonus—your completeness will be a blessing for your future partner.

Myth #7: If You Are Single, You Will Grow Old Alone

This is a crazy myth because whether or not you grow old alone has nothing to do with your marital status. Many married people grow old alone, too. Their spouses may die before them, or their children may live far away. For example, in their later years, my grandparents spent much time alone, and this was not because we never visited them. My parents, aunts and uncles, and we grandchildren spent countless hours at their nursing home, but we could not provide them with round-the-clock company.

Being single does not mean you will grow old alone. Just like married people—like my grandparents—singles often have the companionship of other family members and close friends.

In Luke 2:36-38, the evangelist described how Anna's life did not turn out the way she'd planned. Seven years into her marriage, her husband died. As a childless widow living back in the days of Jesus, she had every reason to be afraid of dying poor and alone, but she chose a different perspective. Anna decided to find her strength in God and so remained in the temple, in God's dwelling place, putting her trust in Him and preaching to His people. She became a fantastic influencer who changed lives by bringing hope. The prophetess lived to the ripe old age of eighty-four and died surrounded by people she'd dedicated her life to helping.

Like Anna, if you honor God first, He will take good care of you, no matter whether you are single or married.

Myth #8: Long-Term Singles Are Unmarried Because Expectations Are Too High

A few years ago, my friend Nathan told me, "When you get older, you've got to lower your expectations if you want to get married." His words bothered me and reminded me of earlier conversations I'd had with Christian friends in which they'd claimed that the unrealistic expectations of single people contributed to their increasing numbers in churches. I didn't believe either of these statements, and, as a scientist, I was happy to find a study confirming my opinions with facts.

Early in 2020, the YMCA University of Applied Sciences in Kassel, Germany, and the research institute empirica, released a study entitled "Lebensweisen christlicher Singles [Lifestyles of Christian Singles]."[1] In it, the authors stated there had been a substantial increase in the number of singles living in Germany. "On average, they are between five and six years without a partner. Every fifth German at this age [18 to 65 years old] has been single for more than 10 years." These numbers tell us that if you have been single for many years, you are in good company.

But what did the researchers say about the underlying causes for the increased number of singles? First, they wrote there was no easy explanation, or in the words of the sociologists, "There is no mono-causal cause for living as a single person." Rather, they observed a combination of social and individual-biographical causes, including factors like these: too close connection to the parents, the inability of singles to commit, and traumatizing bonding experiences. To be fair, they did find evidence that "singles often have exact and diverse expectations of a potential partner and a clear ideal image," but this represented just one possible causal factor in the increased number of singles. Perfectionism and an inferior judgment of "when a relationship has prospects (and then marry) and when not (and then separate in time)" were listed as likely contributing causes, too.

---

1 Künkler T., Faix T., Weddigen J., Beckemeier D., Jäckel M., Merz S., Funke P., Forschungsbericht zur Empirica Singlestudie 2020, *Lebensweisen christlicher Singles*, CVJM Hochschule, 2020.

Rather than being picky about your choice of a life partner, you may remain single because you realize you shouldn't accept every possible relationship that presents itself. It may mean that you say "no" because you know it is not the right time or not the right thing to do. That is a sign of maturity and not a symptom of too-high expectations. When I was in college, I could have dated a wonderful woman, but I gently turned her down because I realized my studies required all my energy and focus. Was it easy? No. But I am grateful I had the guts to say "no" and remain single. I didn't turn her down because I was being overly picky, but rather because I knew that was not the right time for me to be in a relationship.

Myth #9: Singles Are Second-Class People

Religious settings seem to perpetuate the myth that singles are second-class people much more than the secular world. Most modern societies accept that people choose the lifestyle that fits their current ideologies. If you've had enough of living in a relationship, you take some time off and become a single person. It's your choice. In the current you-only-live-once lifestyle, people can choose the kind of relationships they want to experience. Some of them prefer something long-term and stable, while others look for short-term adventures. In the Western world, whether we are in a relationship or not has little impact on how society views us.

In the church, I find the opposite to be true. Since many Christians believe that God's plan for each of us is to be married, they view older singles as some kind of problem that must be solved. Too few Christian families and not enough pastors know how to relate to people like you and me. Because of this, church leaders often avoid giving a single person a place on their board or another high-profile leadership role. As a result, singles tend to be underrepresented in decision-making groups.

The YMCA study came to the same conclusion: "Many Christian singles feel unseen and unappreciated in churches." When Professor Tobias Künkler presented the study to the public, he said, "Singles love the church, but they also suffer from it." He explained that the congregation and even the singles themselves often consider singleness inferior to married life.

What did Paul write about singles in the church?

> *An unmarried man can spend his time doing the Lord's work and thinking how to please him. ... In the same way, a woman who is no longer married or has never been married can be devoted to the Lord and holy in body and in spirit.*
>
> **—1 CORINTHIANS 7:32 & 34 (NLT)**

In other words, we singles have a significant advantage, having more time at our disposal and a greater focus to invest in our relationship with Our Savior. Cherish that.

Too often, we fall into the comparison trap, comparing singles with married people and pointing out the things that make one or the other superior. Instead, we should follow Paul's example and stress unity:

> *There is neither Jew nor Greek, there is neither*
> *slave nor free, there is no male and female,*
> *for you are all one in Christ Jesus.*
>
> **—GALATIANS 3:28**

This means there are no first-class and second-class people. We all have the same value in God's eyes.

GAINING CLARITY ABOUT LIFE WHILE BEING SINGLE

Now that we've identified and debunked many of the confusing myths we've heard about being single, let's look at some of the methods I used to dispel my confusion and gain clarity about my life as a single person.

Method #1: Replace Negative Thoughts with Positive Ones

Why was I confused about my singleness? Logically, I knew I was perfectly all right, and yet emotionally, I did not feel that way. My internal saboteur—as my life coach would call him—was sending me negative messages like these: "You're not good enough. David, you failed. You don't measure up." So, I felt like a failure, and deep down, I believed it, too.

When others spoke to me about being single, I noticed that my negative thoughts became even louder. Whether these people were making me feel small, unintentionally or not, I found myself thinking negatively during our conversations. Then I realized false beliefs I had about myself, such as, "I really am a failure," or "I should be married already," or "There's something wrong with me," were really to blame for these negative thoughts. Once I identified my false beliefs and corrected them, I was able to stop thinking negatively and to replace those thoughts with positive affirmations, such as, "I'm not a failure. I'm different and unique. God has a plan for me."

Do you also harbor false beliefs about yourself that cause negative thoughts? Try to identify them and dispel them. This may take some practice, so don't worry if it takes you a little time to quiet your negative thoughts. Just keep working on it.

In a counseling course I attended, the teacher asked us to make a list of the words that generated bad feelings in us. Once we completed our lists, she said, "Find a positive opposite of the words you have listed." It was a powerful exercise. When we discussed the results, I noticed that although some of us listed the same negative word, often, our positive opposite words were different. Was one or the other better? No. We all had diverse associations and had to find the positive opposite word that resonated for each of us. For instance, for the word "failure," my positive opposite phrase was, "I'm different." I felt it alluded to my creativity and innovative thinking. I liked being different. And that is the way I want to look at my current season of singleness.

To replace confusion with clarity, we must identify the source of our confusion. It may come from a false belief, such as one of the myths mentioned earlier. If you assign this false belief a negative word and then turn it around and identify your positive opposite, you can dispel confusion and gain clarity. Every time that false belief or negative thought pops into your head, pause for a moment, and recall its positive opposite. Say the positive words out loud. Your feelings will change, and you will begin to think about things in a positive light. Or in the words of Paul:

Fix your thoughts on what is true, and honorable, and right, and pure, and lovely, and admirable. Think about things that are excellent and worthy of praise.

—PHILIPPIANS 4:8 (NLT)

Method #2: Share Your Confusions with God

You may get confused about God himself. Why isn't He giving you what you want? It is a complicated question to which I have found no easy answer yet. I do not understand God's choices all the time.

But don't be afraid to tell Him that you don't get it. In Luke 24:13-35, he writes about two of Jesus's followers, who questioned Him and were able to receive clarification about something that had confused them. After His crucifixion, Jesus appeared to the two men on the road to Emmaus and started talking with them. Even though they did not recognize Him right away, they asked Him why the Jewish leaders had been able to kill the Messiah. Jesus explained to them why He had to die and then revealed His identity.

It is all right to feel confused or to have questions. And there is no problem with having doubts either. Take them to Jesus as His followers did. He will give you clarity on what you can do and what you should do. Pray to Him and His plan will be revealed to you in time.

Method #3: Feed Your Mind with Scripture

The Bible teaches us that nothing is wrong with being single long-term like you and me. Even if you don't hear this message at your church or when talking with your friends, do not despair. The truth I find in Scripture enables me to keep my head up when everyone around me is giving me a hard time. Instead, I hold on to what God thinks about me.

For God is not the author of confusion, but of peace.

—1 CORINTHIANS 14:33

Our enemy wants us to stay confused with his chaos, disorder, death, and destruction, whereas God wants to bring clarity into our lives, which He does through His Word. Look at what King Solomon wrote in the Book of Proverbs:

Within these sayings will be found the revelation of wisdom and the impartation of spiritual understanding. Use them as keys to unlock the treasures of true knowledge.

—PROVERBS 1:2 (TPT)

When you feed your mind with Scripture, you will find genuine knowledge, which is to say you will receive clarity.

Method #4: Seek the Perspectives of Friends You Trust

My good friend and mentor, Michael, helped me move forward on this path from confusion to clarity. We had very different life experiences—he married early and now has several grandchildren—and yet he played a pivotal role in helping me feel healthy as a single person. Michael spoke about how to bring courage and hope into my life, helping me come to grips with this truth. While enjoying delicious meals and wine with him, we had many discussions about his life experiences.

Often over dessert, he would share the relationship insights he had gained over years of coaching young couples. I felt blessed to have such a knowledgeable person at my side. His thoughtful advice questioned my beliefs and challenged me to make tough but necessary changes. His words of wisdom became a balm for my heart, helping it to heal from painful breakups. My friendship with Michael reminded me of this Bible verse:

Oil and perfume make the heart glad, and the sweetness of a friend comes from his earnest counsel.

—PROVERBS 27:9

Michael's wisdom and words of encouragement enabled me to gain clarity. My conviction that I am normal despite my singleness has now grown deep roots inside of me, thanks to him. Like me, you will find the kind words of someone you respect prepare a fertile ground for the words of truth you find in Scripture.

DECIDING TO LIVE WITHOUT FULL CLARITY

I used to want full clarity about why I remain single, and I wanted this clarity immediately. I believed my confusion about my marital status would only disappear once I achieved that understanding. But then I gradually realized I didn't need complete clarity right away because I had God, and I could put my trust in Him. I also discovered He does not want to give us full clarity upfront because He prefers that we put our trust in Him. If we need God, we will build a relationship with Him. And more often than we suppose, it's better for us to have only part of the picture anyhow.

After I obtained my master's degree in chemical engineering, I found I liked research and development (R&D) in biotechnology and decided to pursue a Ph.D. in that subject. For two years, I browsed through a myriad of ads for vacant Ph.D. positions in labs all over the world, but despite my intense search efforts, I didn't find a single suitable situation. I gave up, thinking it must not be the right thing for me to do at that time. Then, one day I arrived at work and walked by the job board. I couldn't believe the posting I saw: "Ph.D. position in the R&D department." Immediately, I knew this was the position I'd been seeking. I applied for it and was accepted.

At first, my Ph.D. project went smoothly, but soon I would be grateful that God had only shown me part of the picture upfront. Two months into the project, my professor abandoned me because of contractual problems with the company. What a disaster. Convinced that God was looking out for me, though, I remained calm and found another professor who agreed with my original project outline so that I didn't have to start over. Three years later, I was able to look back on all I gained through that marvelous experience: four publications as a first author, talks at renowned conferences in Europe and the US, and my doctoral degree. Even though I did not have full clarity when I began my search for a Ph.D. position, God eventually guided me to the ideal position for me. And then, when my first professor left, He guided me through that storm, providing me with the direction I needed, when I needed it.

Accept to live without full clarity about every detail of your life as a single person. Our God is good and will provide us with the clarity we need when we need it.

CHAPTER 1: WRAP-UP

In your single season, you may wonder if there is something wrong with you that is causing you to remain single. Perhaps you believe one of the myths told about being single. These myths have the potential to confuse you. Just remember, you are not weird simply because you are single; no relationship status defines whether you're normal. As a single person, you are fantastic, and being single is a good thing.

Here are some tips to help you dispel your confusion: replace negative thoughts with positive ones, share your doubts with God, feed your mind with Scripture, and seek the perspectives of friends you trust. Realize you don't need complete clarity if you trust in Him. He is good and will provide you with a sufficient degree of clarity at the right moment.

CHAPTER 1: TAKEAWAYS
MOVING FROM CONFUSION TO CLARITY

POINTS TO CONSIDER

1. Just because you are single doesn't mean you are a failure, someone with issues, or a person who is crazy and irresponsible. You are normal. No relationship status defines who you are.

2. You can move from confusion to clarity about your singleness by replacing negative thoughts with positive ones, sharing your doubts with God, feeding your mind with Scripture, and seeking the perspective of friends.

3. Accept to live your single season without absolute clarity. Instead, trust in God because He will give you the degree of clarity you need when you need it.

QUESTIONS FOR GROUPS

1. What myths about your single life do you still believe? How do they confuse you? Share these thoughts with the group.

2. How do you plan to gain clarity about your life as a single? Encourage each other to make it happen.

ACTION STEPS TO TAKE

1. On a piece of paper, write, "I am normal. Nothing is wrong with me just because I am still single."

2. Post the note on your fridge or any place you will see it often.

CHAPTER 2

REVISING YOUR SEARCH FOR A SOULMATE

No matter what type of anger or frustration we have to struggle with, ... a clear picture of how our faith in God is the answer to anything we need to overcome.

—CAROL GRAHAM, AUTHOR AND SCHOLAR

STORY OF A SINGLE

I struggled to accept that I had no girlfriend. I kept repeating to myself, "It's unfair to be alone! I deserve someone in my life!" I was frustrated because I was by myself and unable to give my heart to someone. I wanted to take care of someone and share my life with her, side by side. I even dreamed about it.

Then, a few years ago, I realized that I shouldn't ask, "Why am I still alone?" God helped me focus on what I could give instead of concentrating on the spouse I lacked. "Why am I waiting to find my soulmate to begin to give of myself?" I wondered. This realization changed my priorities. I now spend quality time with people and meeting new people. I like attending language exchange meetups and using dating applications. I enjoy meeting women to engage in great conversations instead of searching for Mrs. Right.

And I spend more time with my family. Besides having a good time with them, I find I can express my creativity with them, especially with my ten-year-old niece. I must make a deliberate effort to set time apart for them since my brother's family lives in another city.

I also learned that sometimes I must sacrifice some things that are important to me in order for me to follow God's plan. Recently, I realized I needed to live with someone else, but I had a long-term dream: to have a garden. One day a friend asked me if I wanted to become his flatmate, but he had no yard. I said, "No," because I wanted my garden dream to come true. But then, a few weeks later, I reconsidered my decision, asking myself, "What's more important? A garden or a flatmate?" I decided to sacrifice my backyard—for the moment—and my decision filled my heart with much joy.

Step by step, knowing myself better, and following God's plan, I'm becoming happier and closer to my heart's desire.

—OLIVIER, THIRTY-SEVEN YEARS OLD, SWITZERLAND

A DIFFERENT VALENTINE'S DAY

Today is Valentine's Day. You might be thinking what I used to think: "Oh, no! I have no date tonight, but I don't want to be by myself." I wanted to enjoy a Valentine's Day complete with soft music, a box of fancy chocolates, and a romantic candlelit dinner. But instead, I was sad because I had no date and stayed at home while everybody else was out having a good time.

Being single in our thirties or forties is hard. But there are many ways for us to find joy in our single season.

One Valentine's Day a couple of years ago, two friends and I decided to have a singles' Valentine's dinner. Instead of staying home and thinking about how nice it would be to have a date, we came up with a great alternative: not a pity party but a real party. Did we have a good time? You bet. Kelly invited us to her home, where we cooked a delicious dinner together. Chris brought her flowers and explained he had no intention of hitting on her. The flowers were simply a gift to say, "You're a great single person and a great friend."

We had a great time that evening. We had many interesting discussions about our projects at work, the dream destinations for our next vacations, and design ideas for our future homes. Chris made us all laugh by quoting funny lines from classic movies and our favorite radio comedy show. In no time, I forgot about being single and was glad I hadn't stayed home alone.

Over the years, I have found many other ways to thrive in my season of being single, but I know that there will be many more challenging moments in my future, moments when I become frustrated and tormented by my singleness. And I may still need to survive another lonely Valentine's Day or two. But I know that with some creative problem solving, I can turn around difficult times like those and make them joyful situations.

As you know, being single can be tough sometimes. Let me share some of my unsuccessful attempts to find "the one" for me. Perhaps you can relate to my experiences.

SOME OF MY FAILED ATTEMPTS TO FIND A SOULMATE

In my twenties, I wanted to have a steady girlfriend and felt a little disappointed that I didn't. My friends and I talked about our singleness, expressing our frustrations, but it didn't bother us too much, and we forgot about it most of the time. We had many other exciting things to think about: the next road trip, a crazy hike, or a mountain bike ride. Why not going camping in the nearby woods?

In my early thirties, I was just coming out of my first serious relationship. At first, I was glad to be single again, but then I started to ask myself questions like, "Why are my friends getting married, and I'm struggling to find a date? And why do I have to work so hard to build a meaningful and reliable relationship?" My frustrations grew.

And then one Sunday, I noticed this beautiful, funny, talented, and passionate woman at my brother's church. When she sang on stage, she wore a huge smile, and her voice blew me away. I immediately fell in love with her and lost every bit of rationality I ever had. That day, I managed to meet her and we exchanged a few words—"Hi!" and "See you later!"—but I didn't get to know her the way I wanted to. She, for her part, barely seemed to notice I was alive. Over the next few weeks, I tried to get her attention, which was difficult because I lived in a different city, more than two hours away. I couldn't attend her church meetings during the week, and the weekend services were so crowded, I never got the chance to speak to her alone.

Long story short—I decided to change my strategy. Although it was not Valentine's Day, I decided to pretend it was by sending her a memorable present that would make her realize I was the guy to date. At the time, I was in the army, so one evening, I stood outside our bunker—the only place I could find reception—and typed my entire order on a tiny smartphone screen. I hit "send" just before our supervisor turned out the lights for the night. Looking back, this makes me laugh.

A few days later, my pseudo-Valentine's Day present arrived at its intended destination. The dozen white roses I sent made a big impression on the woman I was in love with—but not in the way I was expecting. My generous and heartfelt gift overwhelmed her. She hated it! She wrote to me and said that one does not send a present like that to someone he hardly knows. "What? Are you serious?" I asked. I was devastated.

Today, I understand I went overboard with the white roses. As an alternative, I should have talked with her more and gotten to know her in advance of sending the flowers. Had I done that, my chances of success would have skyrocketed. Instead, my all-in approach was overpowering. This was one lesson I learned the hard way.

In the aftermath of that disastrous attempt to find my soulmate, I decided to try to form friendships with women I liked but did not want to date. I thought it might be a good way to learn how to be more comfortable around women. That didn't work either, because when I tried to be just friends with a woman, I noticed that sooner or later, she would want our relationship to grow to be a romantic one, and so our friendship would come to an end. I grew tired of starting friendships with women only to have them end abruptly and awkwardly.

One of the few times I did manage to have friendships with women was in a church music group I joined in my thirties. The group consisted of three gals and two guys. We would go out after our band practices each week and have a blast together. We were all creative musicians and were passionate about innovating. We arranged songs to add a new vibe to them, and then jammed for hours, never getting tired. But we were not only a worship band; we became good friends, too, sharing a significant part of our lives.

For me, being in the band was great. It was the first time I managed to have platonic friendships with women. We all laughed together, traveled, went for dinner, and laughed some more over drinks. Our band played together for many months, and most of our friendships continued even after we stopped our band project.

About ten years later, I discovered I might have missed an opportunity for a romantic relationship with one of my bandmates. I ran into another church musician at a retreat, and he said, "David, we all tried so hard to hook you up with Julie. She told us she really liked you, and we all thought you would have been such a great couple."

I was shocked. "It never occurred to me that Julie was interested in me romantically, not even for a single minute." To me, being in the band with her and the other women meant we were friends— nothing more. I enjoyed her company, and I realized we shared many common traits and values, but it did not occur to me there could be anything more with her. Since the band broke up, Julie had married and started a family. Now, I realized I could have been the one she had the family with. I wondered why I had missed that chance. A blend of regret, frustration, and confusion hit me. At the same time, my mind told me that I did not fall in love with Julie for a reason. When we were in the band together, I was in my thirties and had been working in the corporate world for a few years, whereas Julie had just begun her university studies, so there was a substantial age difference between us. A relationship at that time may not have been a good idea. That being said: today, if I had the chance again, I would not hesitate to ask Julie out.

REVISING YOUR SEARCH FOR YOUR SOULMATE

Since I didn't seem to be having much success finding my princess, I decided to take a closer look at my attitudes and methods to determine if I should change anything to increase my chances. After much self-evaluation, I developed this list of six steps to help me in my search for my soulmate. I hope you find them helpful for you, as well.

Step #1: Realize Being Frustrated Is Legitimate

I am frustrated not to have found my soulmate yet. I want a ring on my left ring finger. Being single was never my choice, and it's still not my preferred plan. And yet, I'm not going to allow myself to find just anyone to get into a relationship with because I am frustrated.

My frustration increases when I speak with my married friends who say, "David, your expectations for a girlfriend are too high. At your age, you have to lower your bar." When they say that, I feel as if they do not respect me. But then I remember that these married friends may not understand me or my situation.

My childhood friends and I still get together once or twice a year. We have stayed in contact despite our jobs, busy schedules, and the fact that some of us have moved to different countries all over the globe. I am even more impressed we keep in touch considering our often widely varying viewpoints and politics. Despite these differences, we usually provide each other with valuable support and advice. Today, I am very thankful for our group.

This was not always the case. In the past, there were times I did not want to talk to them because I felt they did not understand me since many of them were now married and had families. I remember feeling this way one time in particular, when I had just broken up with a long-term girlfriend. Some of these friends said I was crazy to break up with her, and one even made that dreaded comment: that I had too-high expectations. I felt they were not trying to see things from my point of view and found their attitudes very frustrating.

As a single person, sometimes, I find it hard to handle the emotional difficulties of being alone. I find it even harder to endure the lack of support, misunderstanding, and ridicule from some of my uninformed friends. I know they don't mean to, but sometimes their comments hurt me. Fortunately, I have always had much support from my family. I hope you enjoy similar support from your family, too. Regardless, please know that there's nothing wrong with feeling frustrated about being single. Being single is frustrating.

Step #2: Come to Grips with Church Frustrations

Have you noticed that many churches fail to relate well with the increasing number of singles in their congregations? Have you wondered why many of them fail to provide support, resources, and activities for their unmarried population? I've often pondered these questions, too.

One Sunday, our local pastor announced, "Next week we won't have study groups. Use this time to spend with your spouse and your children."

When I looked around, it struck me that most of us attending the evening service were single. "Doesn't he see that our church needs to focus more on singles?" I wondered. Then I realized that most of the committee members who made decisions about our church's programs were married and that the married people and our pastor might not know how to tailor programs to meet the needs of long-term singles like me. I wondered, "How can my pastor understand me since he married at a young age? What can he teach me? What does he know about my life?" I figured the married committee members might have similar difficulties trying to understand a single person's perspective.

Another frustration I felt with my church was that because it failed to provide us single people with a sense of community—a place we could call home—many singles eventually stopped coming to church at all. This created even fewer opportunities to get to really know other singles and to develop long-term relationships. Meeting the right person is about finding someone with shared values: someone who serves others, loves the Lord, is faithful, and lives their life with purpose. And where better to find that sort of person than at church? Of course, you might meet such a person in a bar, on an airplane, or in a store. That has happened to many people, but the chances of meeting such a person are much higher in a church. This was why I was even more frustrated with my church for not paying more attention to us single people. I prayed, "God, what's going on? I've been serving in this smaller church for many years. Why can't it provide me with an opportunity to meet my soulmate?" I could have gone the easy way and moved back to my hometown close to Zurich. In the large church my family went to—with more than a thousand people attending the various weekend services—I would have had an excellent chance to find my dream date there. But I wanted to stay at my small, local church.

My friend Grace had a similar experience with the church she went to. She had moved from a city to a smaller town in the countryside. For almost two years, she tried in vain to find a place in her new church where she belonged. She felt excluded by the families who didn't seem to recognize the need to create space for single people. They were already busy with their lives and had a good network of friends and activities. Grace contacted her pastor a few times and shared her needs and frustration, but he failed to affect any meaningful changes, much to Grace's disappointment.

Her story made me think, "She and I are not the only ones in this situation. I bet thousands are facing similar challenges." At that time, I was serving as a community pastor in my free time and decided I wanted to help the thirty- to forty-year-olds in our community feel like they belonged to a church—ours or another one. I told our senior pastor, "We need to create a space for them." Despite my scientific mindset, I did not opt for an extensive study to understand all the underlying factors and possible options. I felt it would take too much time, and the results would end up being too diverse. Instead, I simply created a space where singles and dating couples could meet. It was not limited to any specific target group, but it became successful in no time. "You're doing something vital," people said. These single people often told me that such a group was hard to find. Most of the participants were single, although dating couples would also attend once in a while. When they married, they often moved on to other groups, looking for fellowship with other married couples.

What can you do if you live in a region where you do not get to choose your church because there is only one and the leadership does not understand the struggles of singles? Perhaps you could do as I did and start a singles' group of your own. It may provide you with the community and fellowship you'd like to find in your church—and possibly the opportunity to meet your soulmate.

Step #3: Accept That Being Single Is Difficult Sometimes

Life is full of frustrations, disappointment, and hardships. Everybody's life. No one lives cradle-to-grave without encountering difficulties along the way. As singles, we have to deal with a special set of problems, such as dealing with loneliness, searching for our soulmate, and seeking God's will in our single lives. The good news is that we don't have to cope with these problems alone. God is here to help us through our difficult times.

The shepherd David had many troubles, too. Fortunately for him, he learned in his early years to bring them to God. No disappointment, no doubt, no anger was too big to express to the Lord. David prayed:

I am feeble and utterly crushed; I groan in anguish of heart. All my longings lie open before you, Lord; my sighing is not hidden from you. My heart pounds, my strength fails me; even the light has gone from my eyes.

—PSALM 38:8-10 (NIV)

David's prayers did not bring immediate relief. He had to wait and trust that sooner or later—in God's time—his problems would vanish. Until then, he had to accept that his life may be more difficult than he would like but that God would help him through it.

I find David to be an excellent example for me as a single person. I have always been worried that I won't ever get married. The thought of spending the rest of my life single was too much for me to handle. I tried to ignore it, but I kept worrying anyway. I saw where I was—alone and single—and where I wanted to be—happily married—and how far the two realities were apart, and I became frustrated. So, I prayed to God, asking Him to help me with my problem, and then—like David—I felt God give me the strength to make the best of my life now.

I wrote this book because I care about your life, too. I understand that your expectation gap between being single and being married may steal your joy and make you feel like a failure. You ask the Lord for His help and guidance in finding a soulmate, but when He doesn't answer right away, you might lose hope. Let's be honest: being single sucks sometimes. But if we pray to God, He will help us in His own way and time. And He will give us the strength we need until His help arrives.

Step #4: Focus on the Positive

Over the years, I discovered how to become happy despite not being able to achieve my desire to find my princess. I want to end my single season, which has been going on forever—at least that's how it feels—and enter the wonderful world of relationships, but that has not happened yet. So, what should I do? As this story of the two wolves shows, I have two ways to look at it.

One day, a grandfather tells his grandson a compelling story about two wolves. He looks into

the eyes of the small boy and says, "There are two
wolves inside of us which are always at battle.
One is a good wolf, which represents things like
kindness, bravery, and love. The other is a bad
wolf, which represents things like greed,
hatred, and fear."

The grandson stops and thinks for a second.
Then he looks up at his grandfather and says,
"Grandfather, which one wins?"

The grandfather quietly replies,
"The one you feed."

—TRADITIONAL CHEROKEE TALE

For now, I am single, even though I do not want to be. I don't feel
like I have the gift of singleness. As shown in the story above, I have
two choices: to feed the bad wolf and focus on what's lacking in my life
or to nourish the good wolf and pay attention to all that is good. The
Bible tells us:

> *Take every thought captive to obey Christ.*
>
> **—2 CORINTHIANS 10:5**

In other words, in Christ, we have the power to overcome every negative thought, including frustration. We are not victims. Instead, you and I can choose how we view our circumstances.

This year on Valentine's Day, I decided to focus on maintaining a positive attitude. I sent texts to my single friends, suggesting we have dinner at a nice restaurant in town. I wanted to celebrate that special day—usually reserved for couples—together with my single friends. I could have stayed at home alone, obsessing about still being single, but I decided to feed the good wolf instead and focus on the great friends I have in my life. We enjoyed dinner together at the restaurant and then drinks at a nearby bar afterward. If you had observed us that evening, you would not have noticed any sign of discouragement, despair, or frustration in our faces. Rather we celebrated Valentine's Days in a way that was meaningful to us.

By feeding the good wolf—focusing on the positive—I find sooner or later, my mood improves, and I find joy. Over and over, the Bible teaches us the importance of maintaining a positive attitude:

For as he thinks in his heart, so is he.

—PROVERBS 23:7 (NKJV)

Let us also lay aside every weight, and sin which clings so closely, and let us run with endurance the race that is set before us, looking to Jesus, the founder and perfecter of our faith.

—HEBREWS 12:1-2

I must admit, having a positive attitude while being single has been an ongoing struggle for me. At times, I have been way too focused on my lack of a soulmate. My obsession with singleness even made me wonder if I wanted to get married more than I wanted to follow God's will. I realized that my desire to live in a relationship with a wife had taken on massive proportions that were not healthy; they had become an idol.

Now living in Cambodia, I see with my own eyes what idols are. I see people waving images of lucky cats everywhere. People have altars in front of their houses or in the back of their shops or restaurants. They bow down, burn incenses, and put some food out to pay homage to the lucky cats and calm the evil spirits.

In my singleness, I have sometimes bowed before the altar of fear. I've worried that singleness was inferior to a married person's existence. I also have dreaded regretting my choices later on, thinking, "Maybe I should have asked that woman out. Perhaps she was 'the one' and I missed my opportunity." Paralyzing fear demoralized me. It stole my joy, kept me stationary, and created a chasm between God and me.

Many times I have asked the Lord, "Why am I still single?" but I still have not received a clear answer. That's hard to accept. I don't understand why He is not giving me more information. Hence, I pray, "Help me know what to do. Give me wisdom." I pray for Him to reveal to me His plan for the current season. And, until then, I try very hard to feed the good wolf and maintain a positive attitude.

Step #5: Choose to Rely on God's Goodness

I decided to do something about my frustration so that it was not stealing my joy anymore. I know God is God, and He has the right to decide how and when to answer my prayers. He is sovereign, all-knowing, and yet compassionate. That's why I decided to put my trust in Him. After all, He sent His son Jesus so that we may live our lives to the fullest. This is true, no matter our circumstances. God's plan for each of us now is a single life that overflows. And this life is definitely possible. Indeed, I am experiencing it. I delight in the abundant life that provides me with happiness and satisfaction. It is not a perfect life—

struggles remain—but I feel fulfilled, and that is much more important.

In 1 Samuel 16, we find David's story. He was the youngest of his brothers, and his father did not think the feeble boy would have much success once he grew up. "He can take care of my sheep," he thought. "That's probably all he can manage to do, but at least he will have an excellent occupation and will do meaningful things." He told David, "My son, I'll send you to the pasture to take care of my sheep."

The little shepherd was not thrilled about living out in the fields. "Town is where all the good things happen," he thought. "How will I meet my wife if I'm far away with my father's sheep?" He was right. No girl would take a hike alone that far away from the village. "It's not fair!" David thought. "My older brothers always get to do what they want. They meet the successful businessmen of the town and get to go to their parties." He continued moaning, "Oh, yeah, and they get to meet the good-looking girls at those parties. My father does not treat me well."

Our shepherd boy spent many sleepless nights thinking about the unfairness of his life. He felt unfavored and rejected. In all his turmoil, he decided to tell his sorrows to his Father in Heaven. David believed that God would listen to him and give him the honor and respect his physical father was withholding. His creativity led him to sing his prayers in the form of psalms. If he had lived today, he might have become a famous musical artist by showcasing his songs on *Spotify* or *YouTube*. As it was, he had an audience of only a few dozen: the sheep he took care of, which bleated and scampered in circles around the spotlight artist while he sang. And his Father in Heaven showed up to every concert, proud of the shepherd's sincerity. As David sang his heart out, he rid himself of all his frustrations.

Despite this, the handsome shepherd did not get to meet the

girls or the successful businessmen. Although David prayed to God often, his earthly father did not change his mind. Yet, David left his fear behind, knowing that His Father in Heaven was good. God assured David that he would have a bright future, and that gave him faith.

On the glorious splendor of your majesty, and on your wondrous works, I will meditate. They shall speak of the might of your awesome deeds, and I will declare your greatness. They shall pour forth the fame of your abundant goodness and shall sing aloud of your righteousness. The Lord is gracious and merciful, slow to anger and abounding in steadfast love. The Lord is good to all, and his mercy is over all that he has made.

—PSALM 145:5-9

And so it was, years before David became king—while he was young and single—he understood the story of the wolves. He knew his frustrations, which were rooted in the disappointment that his life was not going the way he wanted, could only be defeated by changing his focus. David realized he had to feed the wolf of faith by trusting in God so that he could live a better life.

This was the turning point for me as a single person. After many years—too many—I concluded that I did not need to wait for the miraculous answer to my prayer for a soulmate. I trusted in God, found hope, and can now rejoice. The revelation that fulfillment does not depend on a relationship status enables me to thrive in my single season.

No matter whether you are single, divorced, widowed, married, with or without children, if you trust in God's love and goodness, you can live your life fulfilled. Period.

Step #6: See Challenges as Opportunities to Grow

As you know, life as a single does not always come easy. Since we can't magically change our marital status, we have to cope with unsatisfied needs and desires, and we must learn to deal with the challenges of single life.

When I was younger, I was scared to death to ask girls out. Because of that, I missed chances to meet some great ones. My fear may have saved me from having to suffer rejection, but it also prevented me from becoming comfortable with women, even as I approached thirty years of age. I finally realized if I wanted to meet women, I would have to get over my fear of asking them out. I saw this challenge as an opportunity to grow, so I clumsily asked out one woman. The next time I asked someone out, I did it better, more smoothly. Bit by bit, one invitation at a time, my confidence grew, and I became much more comfortable with my requests for dates. I faced my challenges and did my best to learn from them.

CHAPTER 2: WRAP-UP

Facing the challenges of our single season can be the best thing that happens to us. Relationships require hard work and patience. Often, a quick fix for marital difficulties is not available. I am willing to endure challenging times while single since it will make me a better husband. Why? From my season as a single person, I already know how to learn from my problems, and thus I'm better equipped to deal with any troubles that might show up in my married season. I changed my mindset and no longer see challenges as problems. Instead, I view them as an opportunity to learn something, to work on me, and to find happiness.

CHAPTER 2: TAKEAWAYS
REVISING YOUR SEARCH FOR A SOULMATE

POINTS TO CONSIDER

1. It is legitimate to feel frustrated about not finding your soulmate yet. Handling the emotional difficulties of being alone and enduring the lack of support, misunderstanding, and ridicule hit our emotions hard. Being single is frustrating.

2. You can't magically change your marital status. Nevertheless, you always have the choice to decide how you look at your circumstances. In Christ, you find the power to overcome every negative thought, including frustration.

3. When you see your single season's challenges as opportunities to grow, you place yourself onto the path to hope, joy, and fulfillment.

QUESTIONS FOR GROUPS

1. How should you revise your search for your soulmate?

2. How can you find hope, joy, and peace despite your as-yet unsatisfied desire to meet your soulmate?

ACTION STEPS TO TAKE

1.   Read Philippians 4:6-7:

Do not be anxious about anything, but in everything by prayer and supplication with thanksgiving, let your requests be made known to God. And the peace of God, which surpasses all understanding, will guard your hearts and your minds in Christ Jesus.

2.   In a journal, write down the steps you feel you should take to overcome your frustrations about being single.

3.   Share this information with someone you trust who will help hold you accountable to take the steps you listed.

CHAPTER 3

OVERCOMING LONELINESS AND FINDING HAPPINESS

But many of us seek community solely to escape the fear of being alone. Knowing how to be solitary is central to the art of loving. When we can be alone, we can be with others without using them as a means of escape.

—BELL HOOKS, AUTHOR, PROFESSOR, AND SOCIAL ACTIVIST

Turn to me and be gracious to me, for I am lonely and afflicted.

—DAVID IN PSALM 25:16

STORY OF A SINGLE

I've been single for ten years. At first, that was by choice, but over time I slowly became aware that I did want someone to share my life with and was ready to seek him out. However, deciding that I wanted a soulmate didn't make him appear.

By this time in my life, most of my friends were married, some with kids. When you get to a place where you find you're the only single person left in the group, it's easy to remove yourself from social situations because you feel like the third or the fifth wheel. I had to force myself to be intentional about building relationships with couples and families. I discovered that we, as singles, can be as good for them as they can be for us. God brought people into my life—families mostly—who welcomed me as their friend. It looked different than I imagined. Friendships in this season meant game nights at home, family BBQs, or sometimes school plays. I loved it. It was a blessing to me in so many ways. I know now it was exactly what I needed at that time. I had to accept that a friendship in this situation looked a little different and embrace it.

Because of these relationships, I didn't struggle with loneliness until I moved abroad. When I first moved, I didn't understand why I felt lonely. I had found a great community I connected with very quickly. But it takes time to create the kind of intimate connections I had spent decades building back home. I realized that you can't just have great friends immediately. You have to welcome people into your life and allow them to see you completely and share all parts of your life. This is real intimacy, which is not just physical. Real intimacy can fight loneliness, but it means having other people who know you deeply and accept you as yourself, which also means you must let yourself be known.

While this is true, physical intimacy is still a need and can be challenging for singles. For me, it's been important to have people in my life that I can be physically close to by finding a friend who knows how to give a great hug just when I need it. Of course, there are still challenges in this area that remain, and there's no easy answer here, but I can say that God knows your needs, and He will meet them somehow, in ways you can't imagine.

Eventually, I realized that maybe in this season, it was okay to feel a little loneliness to remind myself that there is something else for me. While I was blessed with wonderful relationships in my single season, I knew there was still another relationship that I longed for, and it was okay to say, "I'm struggling." It's all right to acknowledge the challenges and feel all the feelings that go with them, but I would encourage you not to stay there too long. There is such a beautiful life to live, no matter your relationship status. There are people you can only reach in this season. There are experiences and opportunities for you to have now that will ultimately make you the person God has designed you to be. There is a plan: His plan. Of course, I still want to find my future partner to share all of these wonderful experiences with. But until then, I'm not going to miss out on the life God has planned for me now.

—STEPHANIE, THIRTY-NINE YEARS OLD, UNITED STATES

Like Stephanie, have you felt alone? Have you wanted to be with someone, to share what you are going through with somebody? I love being with people and enjoy spending quality time with my friends and family, but, as a single, I have struggled with loneliness.

A 2017 study of the psychological well-being of older adults that appeared in The Journal of Marriage and Family concluded that "men seem to suffer more [from] singleness than women. They are psychologically worse off, feel lonelier, have smaller social networks, and hardly any contact persons or confidants. Although quite a few single women suffer from loneliness, they have large networks and more often have close friendships."[2] Regardless of who may suffer more, both single women and men feel lonely.

And yet, as single people, we are not the only ones feeling lonely. People in relationships also experience loneliness. According to the 2020 study from the YMCA University of Applied Sciences mentioned in Chapter 1, "People have a natural need for confirmation, intimacy, appreciation, and security. Whenever these basic needs are not met, a feeling of loneliness arises." Single people tend to believe that being single is the cause of their loneliness due to their inability to share their joys with a significant other.

While growing up, I was involved in many community organizations. My church scout experience as a teenager, and later as a leader, provided me with countless hours of quality time with my friends and with the children I cherished. The close friendships I developed in my church youth group blessed me, too. I was grateful to be a member of these groups, especially when I saw some of my peers leaving the church because they didn't manage to integrate. I was made for such a community, and that's where I flourished. My friends and I discovered that these close friendships formed as young adults strengthened our faith, forged our optimism, and instilled in us a belief that we can improve the world around us. Our community guided our lives, steering us toward success.

As I approached my thirties, however, my communities changed. Some friends moved abroad, and others got married. I moved to the city where I had gone to school and stopped returning to my hometown on weekends. Away from my childhood friends, I became lonely.

---

2 Wright, M. R., & Brown, S. L. (2017). *Psychological Well-being Among Older Adults: The Role of Partnership Status. In Journal of Marriage and Family*, 79(3), 833-849. DDOI: 10.1111/jomf.12375

I didn't know how to meet new people because, in Switzerland, it's almost impossible to get to know someone in a restaurant, café, bar, or even on the street when you're alone. People go out with their friends and usually aren't interested in meeting new people.

My first weekend in the city I now called home, I stayed in my apartment, not knowing what else to do. For what seemed like hours, I walked from my living room to my bedroom and then back again, hoping for inspiration. I watched a few videos on the internet. I even tried to read but didn't get far because my loneliness distracted me. I didn't want my friends to know I was home all by myself when everyone else was in town having fun, so I did something crazy: I deactivated *Skype*, so the green status circle did not light up anymore when I was online.

One weekend alone became two, two became four, and four became dozens of weekends spent by myself and lonely. I dreaded the questions at work on Monday morning: "David, how was your weekend? What did you do?"

I didn't want to say, "I was alone, and it was horrible." What would they think about me?

Then I realized as a single, I had to learn how to spend time by myself, and to enjoy it. In short, I decided if I wanted to live a fulfilled life, I needed to figure out how to overcome loneliness and find happiness regardless of my marital status. Over time, I came up with nine distinct methods to achieve these goals, which I will share with you. I hope some of them may help you, too.

METHOD #1: LEARN TO APPRECIATE SOLITUDE

Some very intelligent people have appreciated the immense value of solitude.

Without great solitude, no serious work is possible.

—PABLO PICASSO

I live in that solitude which is painful in youth, but delicious in the years of maturity.

—ALBERT EINSTEIN

Like these great men, I realized that away from the busyness of community, our empathy replenishes, creative ideas surface, mental strength grows, priorities become clear again, and suddenly we notice God's gentle whisper, saying, "I am with you."

Over time, I discovered the more responsibility I received at work, the more I appreciated my easy-going weekends by myself. Many

Friday nights, I'd arrive home tired and depleted. I didn't want to talk to anyone. I needed space to be alone and replenish my soul. I found many fun ways to enjoy my solitude, too, such as reading, watching inspirational videos, and having private jam sessions on the piano. I also developed the art of relaxation, which had been missing from my young adulthood. And to my surprise, I no longer felt alone when I spent time by myself. I changed my negative perception, comprehending that being alone didn't mean I had to feel lonely.

Fast forward to today: I have completely overcome my fear of being alone. Now I even spend vacations alone, such as the time I traveled solo to Bangkok and Koh Chang island in eastern Thailand. I had a ball. Just a few years ago, such a vacation would have been unimaginable for me, and now I have wonderful memories of a life-changing trip.

However, I do understand I need to balance my alone time with the time I spend with others. Staying alone is safe. Nobody bothers me, and I get to choose what I want to do without having to consider someone else's desires. That makes life much more comfortable. But please don't be afraid—I am not becoming a solitary caveman. Nor will I encourage you to hide in a cave, either. I certainly still enjoy quality time with others and recognize its value in my life. Rather, I've learned to strike a balance between spending time with others and time spent in solitude. Both are important, enjoyable parts of my life, now.

METHOD #2: REALIZE THAT YOU ARE NOT ALONE

Recently, I attended a party at my brother's place, where I was reminded that I'm different. Nobody mentioned it. Nonetheless, pretty much everybody at the party was in a relationship, and most of them already had kids. This highlighted the truth: I was alone and didn't fit in. In moments like that, I struggle with this verse:

Then the Lord God said, "It is not good that the man should be alone; I will make him a helper fit for him."

—GENESIS 2:18

How does this Bible verse apply to me? Does it mean I am not complete as a single? But, wait a minute, consider this verse:

Behold, the virgin shall conceive and bear a son, and they shall call his name Immanuel [which means, God with us].

—MATTHEW 1:23

With this statement, Jesus promised we are never truly alone. No matter what your social media relational status states—single, married, divorced, or whatever—God is with you. It became real when He sent His only beloved son Jesus to be with us on Earth.

You may ask, "Are you serious? Am I really never alone? Even now, when everybody has found their Mrs. or Mr. Betterhalf?" The answer is, "Yes." God said that it wasn't good for us to be alone. And then, in His grace, He provided a way we would never truly be alone. He made us a promise: God sent His son, Emmanuel, who is with us. And we have the Holy Spirit living within us, too.

Let this idea sink in: through His son, Jesus, and the Holy Spirit, God has provided constant companionship and assistance for all of us, regardless of our marital status.

God is our life-giver and foundation, and we depend on Him. Without Him, we lack purpose. When we do not recognize His presence in our lives, we may look for a substitute. When I am not careful, I look for a girlfriend to fill the void inside of me. But then I remember, only God can complete us because He knows us much better than we know ourselves. He knows our deepest feelings, needs, and longings. We need Him. We can be sure that He will never leave us or forsakes us. Hence, we are never truly alone.

METHOD #3: BELIEVE INTIMACY IS POSSIBLE AS A SINGLE PERSON

A friend and I were discussing topics I should use for blog articles, and she asked me, "David, in your life as a single person, how do you cope with the lack of physical touch?" She told me one of her love languages—the ways she felt intimate with others—was physical contact and said she missed it a lot as a single.

I struggled to find a satisfying answer for her. My first love language is spending quality time with people. Physical intimacy does not come naturally to me as I am not inclined to it. For instance, I have a friend who gives me an intense and long hug every time we meet—so strong my ribs almost break. I like it, but I would never do such a thing when meeting other friends because I express my affection through my total presence with them. As a single person, the absence of physical touch is not my biggest concern. I have learned to live without it. But physical touch may be one of your forms of intimacy, and you may crave someone to hold your hand or put their arm over your shoulders and may wonder how to find intimacy as a single person.

In our singleness, I find we need to become creative in creating intimacy because every one of us needs it. If you love physical touch like my friend, as a single, you may feel it is lacking. Likewise, I have missed having someone special with whom to have meaningful conversations—my love language. When I get to spend quality time with someone, such as sharing a delicious dinner in a cozy restaurant, then I thrive. I thrive because I am being intimate with somebody else and feel loved.

No matter how we experience love, intimacy is an integral part of our human nature. We have emotional needs in any season of our lives and need other people. The question is: how can we, as single people, make sure our emotional tank remains full? In other words, what can we do to satisfy our needs for intimacy?

"Wait a second!" you may say. "Isn't this why I should find my soulmate as soon as possible—to have intimacy?" For too long, I believed I could find real intimacy only when I was in a dating relationship. Now I realize that is not true. God can meet any need we may have: physical touch, quality time, or words of affirmation. He promised this to us. I have witnessed Him fulfilling this promise, and so have other single people.

Jesus, God's one and only Son, was single while living on this earth. You may say, "But He is special because He is divine." That is true. Yet, despite His 100 percent godly nature, He was also 100 percent human, and thus faced the same needs and challenges you and I do. He must have felt alone, misunderstood, and not considered, too. And since He experienced this same lack of intimacy, Jesus understands your struggles.

For we do not have a high priest who is unable to sympathize with our weaknesses, but one who in every respect has been tempted as we are, yet without sin.

—HEBREWS 4:15

Jesus could have looked for a woman. Instead, He nurtured a meaningful relationship with His Father in Heaven. As we read in John 10:10, "The Son of God came to bring abundant life." And He lived His life to the fullest, experiencing complete fulfillment despite the potential lack He could have felt looking at married people like his dear friend Peter. This is a crucial lesson: Jesus showed us His solid and profound relationship with His Father enabled Him to enjoy an abundant life ... without a spouse.

Often as singles, we feel we need a relationship, which causes us to focus on what we're missing and to yearn for a soulmate. Our need for an intimate relationship is legitimate, yet the solution we are seeking is wrong.

As singles, we experience a longing for sexual intimacy. I, for one, have not found a magical button to switch off this desire, and I want to avoid giving you stereotypical Christian answers that sound nice, but at the end of the day, do not help much. The challenge is to acknowledge the need for this type of intimacy and to deal with it without resorting to solutions like pornography or sexual intimacy outside of marriage. It's difficult but possible. How? With God's help. Alone I would fail, but His grace gives me the strength to deal with this tension. I take my needs to God, and while sometimes the physical longing remains, I feel inner peace. As a bonus, I learn to gain a broader perspective on what truly makes me happy.

Although we are body, soul, and spirit, I tend to focus on my physical needs. Because of this, I sometimes forget that if I look only for physical relief, my soul and spirit will suffer. My overall well-being must take priority over the short-term satisfaction of physical intimacy for me to thrive. God does meet our needs as He promised He would. We just need to trust Him and hold onto Him, knowing that He is with us in these challenging moments.

Looking back, I see God's hand on my life, helping me deal with a lack of physical intimacy. But it's a constant battle. Paul was conscious of this difficulty, saying:

Flee from sexual immorality.

—1 CORINTHIANS 6:18

God gives us the strength to fight immorality, but sometimes, we may need to take action and consciously avoid luring temptations.

Jesus did not try to find His love in another person. He knew that the Divine relationship was the only way to fulfillment. Jesus called God "Abba," which means "Father." And He began the Lord's Prayer with the words, "Our Father in Heaven." This reminds us that each of our requests should begin with us acknowledging who our Father is—God—and that, as our Father, He has promised to meet our needs.

Did you notice in the opening of the Lord's Prayer, Jesus said, "*our* Father?" That includes you and me, too. We get to build an intimate, consistent, loving, and caring relationship with the Creator of the Universe. As our Father, nothing stops Him from loving us and giving us what we need. Through prayer, we find authentic intimacy that surpasses our physical and emotional needs. Why? Because God provides us with supernatural intimacy, which is the reason prayer is so important. I need to remind myself of this fact often because praying doesn't come naturally to me.

It takes me a lot of effort, and I often fall asleep while praying, but I keep praying because I know building my relationship with my Father in Heaven fills any voids in my life. Any other source of intimacy is counterfeit.

God's dream is to give us an abundant life, which includes emotional and physical closeness. On a recent retreat to Southern Cambodia, I watched the tropical rain creating tiny ripples as it splashed onto the surface of the Kampot River and overflowed the riverbanks. As I enjoyed the beautiful view, I felt God remind me He wanted to bless me with abundant intimacy during my season as a single. We don't need to be satisfied with only a few drops of intimacy, because when we abide in God, we receive the real deal—an abundant tropical rain of intimacy that fills up our hearts until they overflow.

METHOD #4: UNDERSTAND THAT GOD CARES AND WILL MAKE UP FOR ALL YOU LACK

When we experience God's closeness, we also are assured He cares. And that is when our fear of what's lacking will disappear. We can rest easy, knowing that God will compensate us for anything missing in our lives.

As singles, this knowledge of God's compensation can help us prepare for marriage. No spouse—not even the best one we could ever imagine—can satisfy all our needs and give us what we need when we need it, night and day. Such expectations are not realistic and would put enormous pressure on him or her. We will have much better marriages if we learn to go to God with our worries and rely on Him to provide us with whatever we may be missing. And your future spouse will appreciate that you did.

Also, knowing our Father cares about us makes us more relaxed. We will face many issues—big and small—as both single and married people. If we learn to rely upon God's provision in any area of our lives, we can stop worrying because we know He will care for us tomorrow, next week, next year, and twenty years down the road. His love and caring never waver.

In the Bible, David came to that same conclusion, too, and recorded it for future generations to read:

> *I sought the Lord, and he answered me and*
> *delivered me from all my fears.*
>
> **—PSALM 34:4**

METHOD #5: REALIZE THE IMPORTANCE OF COMMUNITY

God lives in a perfect community: Father, Son, and Holy Spirit. God created us in His image, which means that, like Him, we flourish living in a community. We need each other. Life in isolation is not living; it's merely surviving.

During a visit to New York City, I made a surprising discovery about being in a community. I went to a service at Hillsong Church in downtown Manhattan. In the middle of the service, the MC paused the program and said, "We're now going to have four minutes of forced fellowship."

I had never heard of such a thing.

"We're doing this because it's perhaps your only chance this week to meet someone new. We all know New York City can be a busy and lonely place."

The ushers handed out cookies, and the forced fellowship commenced. I chatted with a graphic designer sitting next to me. Although her fashionable clothes made her look like someone who was successful and had many friends, she seemed lonely.

On the way home, I thought about this experience. I would have never imagined finding loneliness in such a big city where you can meet people everywhere. It seemed contradictory that the more people lived in a place, the more they felt lonely.

God loves to plug us into a community. At the beginning of the Bible, we read that He spent the evenings walking in the Garden of Eden, visiting the first humans. God did not place Adam and Eve in the garden to live alone in isolation. Instead, He wanted them to live life together, and He walked alongside them and took part in their lives, too. Living together in a community is part of our human DNA.

As single people, we have fewer opportunities for intimacy than married couples do. If we want to thrive as single people, we have to force fellowship by reaching out and developing friendships with other men and women in our communities.

One way to accomplish this is by eating meals with others. Too often, we run to the nearest fast-food restaurant. Or worse, we buy something at the drive-through. We don't spend enough time eating together, even though Scripture reminds us of the value of a shared meal. Jesus even spoke about a heavenly dinner, saying He is preparing a feast for us that will put us in a state of awe and wonder. Sounds like it will be delicious!

In my own life, I have seen the value of breaking bread together. I fondly remember the hour-long Sunday lunches I had with my parents. Even as teenagers and then young adults, my two brothers and I would open up and talk about whatever was on our minds. On those Sundays, we had plenty of time, and so did my parents, so we ate, and we talked—about anything. And we laughed.

My brothers and I especially loved it when our dad would talk about his youthful escapades. I remember one time, he leaned forward and said, "Boys, one afternoon, my brothers and I were pulling a trailer with our tractor." He couldn't hide his smile. "As we drove down the hill outside the village, I shifted the tractor into neutral to speed up."

Looking at each other, my brothers and I said, "Tell us more!"

"We wanted it to go faster, and it did. In the beginning, it went well, but then, when I wanted to slow down, the brakes overheated so much they started to smoke. Luckily, we managed to pull over and stop seconds before the brakes would've given out altogether. Before continuing, we had to pack the brakes with snow to cool them down."

We learned a lot about our dad through stories like that. Afterward, we would talk while my mom served us delicious desserts with a smile. And then we'd go right on talking.

That is community: spending life together. I wonder what Adam and Eve told God as they walked through the garden in the cool of the day. And what about our Father in Heaven? What did He say? I'm sure He told them how proud He was of them like any good father does to his children.

As singles, we know we need community. It is crucial to spend quality time with other people, but achieving it is not always easy. We need to intentionally seek community because we cannot thrive without sharing our lives with others.

METHOD #6: RECOGNIZE THE COMMUNITY OF THE CHURCH

The amazing community of the first church impresses me. At Pentecost, the people in Jerusalem were amazed and perplexed because they heard the believers talking in other languages. Peter spoke to the crowd and explained what was happening. Through his sermon, the people understood that they were witnessing the fulfillment of ancient prophecy: the outpouring of God's Spirit. Luke recorded this in the Book of Acts:

Now when they heard this, they were cut to the heart, and said to Peter and the rest of the apostles, "Brothers, what shall we do?"

—ACTS 2:37

God touched the locals and the foreigners alike, who heard the good news for the first time in their own language. That day alone, 3,000 repented and were baptized. This community of believers became the first church. It was so alive. The church members shared so much of their lives with each other. Imagine their ongoing laughter, smiles, hugs, taps on the shoulder, words of encouragement, and genuine affection. It was not a single event or a social media selfie to impress friends and family; they experienced authentic community as their way of life.

> *And day by day, attending the temple together and breaking bread in their homes, they received their food with glad and generous hearts.*
>
> **—ACTS 2:46**
>
>

We can learn a lot from the vibrant community of the first church. They walked and talked with each other, and they laughed and cried while sharing meals that lasted for hours.

When I visited Mosaic, a vibrant church in Hollywood, California, I saw how powerful a modern church community can be. Mosaic created a culture where anyone can belong to the church, even before they believe. And Mosaic strives to create a home for anyone in the city who doesn't have one. Hundreds of people hung out on the church's veranda in front of its entrance. Mosaic felt so vibrant and alive—like a gathering of a big family or good friends who were glad to see each other again after a long absence. That was such a refreshing experience for me that filled up my soul, and made my loneliness vanish.

That is what we need: a real community. And often, a good place to find a real community is a church.

METHOD #7: LEARN TO LEVERAGE TECHNOLOGY

In this age of social media, you would think single people would have an easier time connecting and forming a sense of community. Unfortunately, in many situations, the opposite seems to have happened. We have unlearned how to talk to each other.

Perhaps this sounds familiar: A friend calls you, but you don't answer the phone. Instead, you text him a few seconds later, ask him what he wants, and, if you are interested, you call him back. Why do we do this? Are we afraid of spending too much time connecting with other human beings? Could it be that social media pushes us away from real connections?

It bothers me that sometimes I choose to be alone to avoid dealing with other people. At these times, my isolation is a choice I'm making. However, some of you may feel isolated because you are afraid to meet other people. You realize reaching out into the community would be fulfilling, but know it takes a lot of courage to put yourself out there, and sometimes that effort may seem overwhelming. In this situation, social media might be helpful to you. Rather than using social media and technology to further isolate yourself, consider using it to forge new connections.

During the COVID-19 pandemic, when our respective governments required us to stay home, many single people found a new meaningful way to connect through videoconferencing. At first, I was afraid to launch an online hangout myself because I wasn't sure I could do it well. I worried, "Will people like it? Can I engage them in an open and proactive conversation? Will I find it weird to connect with people I've never met in person?" But eventually, I did start up a virtual hangout and, after our first session, we all concluded it was a success and that we would meet again soon. We discovered chatting online was a great way to communicate with others, especially during that particular time.

Why not take a chance—or two—to meet other people? I am sure many other singles are waiting for someone to reach out to them. Let's be the ones who make the leap of faith and grab the phone or send a link to connect.

METHOD #8: CHALLENGE YOURSELF TO FIND A COMMUNITY THAT'S NEW TO YOU

Knowing God walks alongside us can give us the strength and courage we need to join a community that's new to us. Sometimes, we need to be creative in finding one where we feel we belong.

While watching Swiss TV one night, I came across a show about Pelle, author of the book *Ich bin Single, ich bin frei* (*I'm Single, I'm Free*). In the interview, he said that although he was afraid that he would be considered weird, he believed God wanted him to live as a single person in a community with married people and then share his experiences with others through writing a book about them. By accepting this challenge, Pelle was able to find a new, unlikely, community where he belonged.

I enjoy being part of a church small group. In that setting, I experience intimate moments in the presence of God and my peers. Oftentimes we begin these small group sessions by sharing a meal. I've had many encouraging, funny, exciting, and touching conversations at that dinner table. For instance, I remember one evening we were eating raclette, a traditional Swiss cheese dish made by pouring melted cheese over a few small potatoes. Lisa, one of the members of our group, caught my eye. With a smile—but without saying a word—she made me understand that we were about to have an eating contest.

"I'm in!" I said.

We bolted one cheesy potato slice after another while toasting our glasses filled with white wine and laughing like crazy. I don't remember who won the contest, but I do remember having a great time. Afterward, with our stomachs over-full, the group made plans to go hiking in the Alps—and to have another raclette contest.

I encourage you to think about what community you can plug yourself into. Can you join a church group? Or perhaps you'd like to share your apartment with other people. Would it make sense to join a fitness club? Or are there one or two people you want to develop a stronger friendship with? Maybe pause for a couple of minutes now and reflect on some practical steps you can take to connect to a community that's new to you.

CHAPTER 3: WRAP-UP

We can find intimacy and closeness, no matter our relationship status: single, married, or divorced. And when we understand that the quality and quantity of intimacy we experience does not depend on another person, but rather on our relationship with God, we can relax. Neither you nor your future spouse is responsible for completely satisfying each other's needs. That's God's job. Authentic intimacy is at your disposal if you put God first. The Bible promises that when we call the name of Jesus, He will call us children of God. And our Father in Heaven takes good care of us. He blessed us with His son Emmanuel—God with us—and promised we would never be alone.

And behold, I am with you always,
to the end of the age.

—MATTHEW 28:20

By trusting in God, we can overcome loneliness and find happiness in our single season. Sounds like a good deal to me.

CHAPTER 3: TAKEAWAYS

OVERCOMING LONELINESS AND FINDING HAPPINESS

POINTS TO CONSIDER

1. Overcoming loneliness seems daunting at first. However, if you learn to appreciate solitude, you will discover its great value. Away from the busyness, our empathy replenishes, creative ideas surface, and priorities become clear again.

2. Although you may feel lonely, you are not alone. God is with you all the time. His supernatural nature lets you experience His closeness.

3. If you want to thrive, recognize the importance of being part of a community. In your singleness, make it a priority to develop friendships with other men and women, become part of a church group, and spend time with families.

QUESTIONS FOR GROUPS

1. How do you overcome your feelings of loneliness and lack of intimacy?

2. What ways to connect with other people have you found effective and fulfilling?

3.   Where do you struggle in your quest to develop friendships?

ACTIONS STEPS TO TAKE

1.   List five creative ways to reach out to new people.

2.   Try one of these ways today.

CHAPTER 4

DISPELLING FEARS AND FINDING CONFIDENCE

Be strong and courageous. Do not be frightened, and do not be dismayed, for the Lord your God is with you wherever you go.

—JOSHUA 1:9

Confidence is created by the small things you do every single day that build trust in yourself.

—MEL ROBBINS, TELEVISION HOST AND MOTIVATIONAL SPEAKER

STORY OF A SINGLE

When I was in high school, my first girlfriend hurt me a lot. She ended our relationship to be with another guy. It was sudden, and I didn't see it coming. I felt betrayed, and it affected the way I looked at myself. Because it didn't work out with her, I was afraid that other girls I asked out would reject me, too. Not wanting to be hurt again, I stopped taking risks.

I sometimes worry that I might never find my life partner. Will I end up being alone and even die alone? The more time goes by, the more I wonder if I'll ever have the chance to find my soulmate. The challenge I have is that when I meet a woman, I find 10,000 reasons in my head that it's not worth trying: she's too pretty for me, I'm not handsome enough, not tall enough, not smart enough, or any other excuse I find not to approach her. There's no logical thinking behind this self-sabotage. It's biased—based on negative experiences. Sometimes I even think I'm cursed: I won't find love, and I'll never be happy. My past failures resulted in a lack of self-confidence and impacted my ability to approach and date women confidently. If I were more self-confident, I wouldn't have such an issue inviting a date out for a coffee.

Letting go of my bad past experiences was key to moving forward. I decided to focus on how I could improve myself rather than dwelling on what's wrong with me. Also, I learned not to compare myself with others. That's the biggest mistake you can make.

What helps me is to compare myself with a previous version of myself. Three years ago, I was burnt out and stressed, and I didn't connect with God regularly. I didn't journal, had no written goals, ate junk food several times a week, and didn't work out. I decided to do my best to improve as many of those problems as I could. As I got better, I became more confident. Now, when I doubt myself, I remind myself of the progress I've made, and I remember God's promises.

I can't control when I'll meet my future wife, and I don't know who she'll be. But I can do everything I can to become a better version of myself, the best husband my future wife would like to have.

—PHIL, THIRTY-TWO YEARS OLD, FRANCE

The biggest mistake I made while single was spending too many years thinking I was weird and had issues to resolve. I am not saying I'm perfect—far from it. My point is I was putting my entire focus on trying to fix my faults, thinking that was the only way I'd ever be able to have a meaningful relationship with a woman. My negative view of myself made me feel increasingly anxious. "There must be something wrong with me," I thought. "I can't manage to sustain a relationship." I tried counseling, but even with professional help, I couldn't find the root of my problem—what was causing me to remain single.

One cold autumn evening, my friend Erwin prepared raclette, which, as you already know, is one of my favorite dishes. As he was pouring the melted cheese over the warm potatoes, he said, "David, I don't get why I can't stay in a relationship."

"I'm wondering the same thing about myself," I said.

He said, "I keep trying to identify what's wrong with me—why I can't get a girlfriend—but I can't figure it out."

My conversation with Erwin made me realize other singles felt the same way I did. But, here's the thing: even though you and I may think that we stay single because we are flawed and in need of fixing, that is not what I have observed. When I served as a community pastor at my local church, I met many singles who were amazing people. I'm sure you're great, too. The fact is single people are not any more messed up than married or divorced people. So, why do we feel insecure—like there is something wrong with us?

DISPELLING FEARS

Could the insecurity we are experiencing stem from fear? As the COVID-19 wave hit around the globe, a wave of fear overwhelmed my social media feed. It was as if many were afraid the world would end any minute. In my home country of Switzerland, people emptied grocery stores, irrationally hoarding items like toilet paper, because of fear.

What happened during this crisis made me think about my singleness and made me realize my worries about my marital status came from various irrational fears. Because of these fears, I felt insecure and doubted myself. To conquer these fears, I identified and examined each one individually. I hope you may benefit from the following look at some of the fears I had about being single.

Fear #1: Time Is Running Out

In my late twenties and thirties, I was in a rat race. I thought there wasn't enough time to do all I had to do and always felt like I was running late.

This feeling of running out of time started with my career. After graduating from university, I struggled to find a job. For nine months, I was unemployed, and then for another two years, I went from one temporary six-month contract to another. Because of my slow start, I felt my friends were more advanced in their careers, and I needed to run faster and work harder to catch up.

I had the same type of feeling regarding my singleness. I saw friend after friend get married, and yet I remained single. I worried I might not be able to catch up to them. I calculated how long it would take me to meet someone, date her, get married, and then build a life together—hopefully with children—and became afraid I was running out of time. My fear led me to date as many different women as possible, which prevented me from getting to know any one of them very well. This was not a good way to find a soulmate. How could I possibly know if I have much in common with a woman after just one or two dates? My fear of running out of time was preventing me from fully exploring those potential relationships.

Fear #2: I Am Missing Out

I saw many of my friends find their prince or princess, get married, and then experience the joys of family life. It made me worry about how I would feel if I turned forty or fifty and was still unmarried and waiting for my family life to begin. Would I regret missing out on the experiences my friends were having? Would I feel like a loser because I did not get to enjoy the richness of a life of two-ness? Rather than living my single life to its fullest, I was spending too much time observing my married friends and being envious of what they had.

Now, I don't think I will miss out just because I've stayed single longer than my friends. God may still provide those experiences to me, or perhaps He will send different opportunities my way. I need to trust Him and feel fulfilled, regardless of whether or not I get married. To quote Abraham Lincoln, "And in the end, it's not the years in your life that count; it's the life in your years."

Fear #3: I'm Making the Wrong Choices

I often doubted myself and the choices I made. Maybe I should have called that fair-haired woman I met on the train in Zurich. Or perhaps I should have given that sweet gal in my church group another chance. I thought I had made poor decisions, and my friends had made good ones because they were all married with families, which I believed was superior to my life as a single person.

But the Bible does not support this myth. As we saw in the first chapter, Paul remained single, but that did not mean he had made a mistake. On the contrary, he certainly lived a fulfilled life as shown by the powerful mark he left on the church world. Paul followed the path God prepared for him and thrived. I, on the other hand, was second-guessing my every decision rather than seeking the guidance of my Father. I needed to follow Paul's example of trusting God—and myself.

Fear #4: My Expectations for a Soulmate Are Unrealistic

Did my expectations for my soulmate exceed the norm? Was that why I had not found my future wife yet? Counseling helped me to sort through this type of question. And then I brought my expectations before God, asking Him to show me how to edit my list of spousal requirements to make it more reasonable. To my surprise, I concluded that in some areas, I actually should increase my expectations for some core values, not lower them. This contradicted my friends who recommended compromises.

Could it be that because we think we are running out of time—getting closer to that forty-year-old mark—we doubt we are on the right track when looking for a soulmate? I am not advocating unrealistic expectations. Instead, I examined my feelings to discover what attributes I most wanted in a future spouse. I paid particular attention to the core values I was seeking, realizing those were the most important. (More about that in Chapter 11.) At the same time, I recognized the success of my future relationship would not depend on the less important traits I had listed, and so I put less emphasis on them in my search. However, more than anything, I realized that I needed to open my heart and mind to God more and to allow Him to guide me in my choices.

Fear #5: God Is Not in Control

As a community pastor, I had countless discussions with other singles that went along these lines:

- Aimee was disappointed Tom did not take the initiative. She said, "I feel like single Christian men aren't brave enough."

- John said that he didn't understand why the woman he was in love with did not want to go out with him.

- Vanessa asked, "Am I not beautiful anymore? No guy is interested in me right now, and I'm getting worried I'll miss out on having a family and children. My biological clock is ticking."

In all of these situations, my response was, "Don't worry. God has everything under control." I honestly thought I believed that too: *God will take care of everything. Always.*

But then I noticed I often tried to handle my own problems myself, without first seeking His guidance. I examined why this was and realized that deep inside my heart, I did not fully trust God to handle things for me. Although I did not hesitate to comfort others with this truth, when I dealt with my own situations, doubts kicked in, coupled with thoughts that maybe God was too busy to help me, and maybe I wasn't important enough to Him. This had to change.

The Bible contains many stories that teach us about trusting God. In the Book of Judges, we find the story of Gideon, who was so determined to win a battle, he amassed a huge army. But God wanted him to do things differently:

The Lord said to Gideon, "You have too many warriors with you. If I let all of you fight the Midianites, the Israelites will boast to me that they saved themselves by their own strength."

—JUDGES 7:2 (NLT)

God told Gideon to cut back the size of his army and assured Gideon that He'd help him win anyway:

The Lord told Gideon, "With these 300 men, I will rescue you and give you victory over the Midianites. Send all the others home."

—JUDGES 7:7 (NLT)

Gideon had no choice; he had to trust God. In the end, God enabled the Israelites to defeat the Midianites despite using a much smaller army.

Like Gideon, I realized God has everything under control, and I need to trust Him more. He wants to help me because I'm important to Him. And so are you. God is telling us all, "I can handle your situation. Let Me do it."

FINDING CONFIDENCE

Doubt kills more dreams than failure ever will.

—BRIAN TRACY, MOTIVATIONAL SPEAKER AND AUTHOR

It happened one morning: The sun rose, with the first beams peeking through the huge leaves of the palm trees, and a few birds sang as a beautiful new day began. A scene like this normally would leave me in awe and give me a sense of peace. But this morning, I could not rejoice. My discouragement sucked out every trace of my hope and joy as I asked God, "Where are you in my singleness?" I was in total desperation, doubting all my choices, and feeling more and more insecure. With a voice full of despair, I said, "Show me what I should do because I can't figure this out by myself. I need Your help."

The next moment I sensed His whisper, saying I should trust Him because He did have a plan for my life. I did not receive any details on how and when this plan would happen, but hearing His promise was enough to give me confidence.

I often looked for words that inspired confidence, expecting to find the right answers in self-help books or inspirational videos. I also consulted the people around me, who offered many opinions about long-term singles over the age of thirty and gave me advice concerning what I should do about being one of them. Most of what they said did not help me much.

After much searching, I generated my own self-help list of lessons to learn to help me gain confidence in myself so I could use this confidence to help me find fulfillment in my life as a single. I've listed these lessons below.

Confidence Lesson #1: Realize God Believes in You

I have to admit, when seeking confidence, my first thought was not to turn to God. I opened the Bible for guidance only when I had exhausted most other resources. But when I finally did turn to Scripture, I found real answers in His Word.

For instance, in Deuteronomy 31:1-8 and Joshua 1:1-9, Joshua's story helped me understand that God provides us with the courage and confidence we need exactly when we need it.

One day when Moses had grown old, he said to his apprentice, "Joshua, I won't enter the promised land."

Joshua looked astonished.

Moses said, "Because you followed my footsteps during the forty years in the desert, you are going to lead the Israelites into Canaan. Your day will come."

At the time, Joshua didn't understand the full gravity of his new role. When his day did come, Joshua panicked, asking, "How am I going to lead the people? I'm not qualified!" Before this, Joshua had been a confident guy, always ready to fight for what was right. Not this time. Faced with his new leadership position, his knees shook, his heart sank, and relentless waves of self-doubt crashed over him. The once confident young man lost his courage.

God told Joshua:

*Moses my servant is dead. Now therefore arise,
go over this Jordan, you and all this people, into
the land that I am giving to them,
to the people of Israel.*

—JOSHUA 1:2

In response, I picture Joshua saying, "No, God. How can I do that? I'm not capable."

God continued:

*Every place that the sole of your foot will tread
upon I have given to you, just as I promised to
Moses. No man shall be able to stand before you
all the days of your life. Just as I was with Moses,
so I will be with you. I will not leave
you or forsake you.*

—JOSHUA 1:3, 5

Despite God's reassurance, Joshua still had doubts, so He said, "Listen to me, Joshua. You are strong and courageous."

Joshua thought, "Strong and courageous? I'm everything except that. Why is God entrusting me with this overwhelming responsibility? He must not be able to see my flaws." He closed his eyes and saw visions of fortified cities, chariots, skilled soldiers armed to the teeth, and giants. He was not sure if he was seeing reality or the trailer of the latest Tarantino movie. In his sleep state, he heard this:

> *Be strong and courageous, for you shall cause this people to inherit the land that I swore to their fathers to give them.*
>
> **—JOSHUA 1:6**

Joshua sat up and touched his aching head, asking, "Where am I? Oh, I must have been dreaming. Did I hear God's voice?" He looked up into the sky and heard a whisper:

> *[Joshua] be strong and courageous. Do not be frightened, and do not be dismayed, for the Lord your God is with you wherever you go.*
>
> **—JOSHUA 1:9**

He waved his hand and said, "I get the point!" Since now Joshua had heard the same message from God three times, he believed Him. God had given Joshua the confidence he needed to lead His people into Canaan.

I can relate to Joshua because, as a single person, I have had self-doubt I needed to overcome. Now, when I need a shot of confidence, I remind myself that God believes in me. For example, while writing this book, I had many attacks of self-doubt. Writing a book is no simple task, and I struggled to believe I could pull off such a challenging project. I soon discovered crafting a book to encourage single people while being transparent about my struggles is a more demanding endeavor than I ever imagined. But, when my self-doubt got the better of me, I often referred back to Joshua's story and received the boost of confidence I needed from God's Word.

Confidence Lesson #2: Modify Negative Thoughts

God repeated His words to Joshua three times so that he could meditate on His promises and thus shift his thinking from negative to positive thoughts. Likewise, I read the vision statement I wrote for this book every day to reaffirm the fact that my plans would come to pass. Whenever I read my vision statement, my energy changed. All of a sudden, I was excited about the impact the book would have on other people's lives. And this excitement permeated my writing, too.

In this same way, you and I can overcome our self-doubt and insecurity about being single. We must remember our thoughts play a pivotal role in overcoming self-doubt. We have a constant war going on in our minds: we can either listen to our negative thoughts and be defeated or refute them with positive thoughts and confidence. Like many people, self-doubt is deeply rooted in my brain, but I am not a victim of my thoughts. I know I can influence what I am thinking.

The Bible says we can submit all our thoughts to Jesus:

[We] take every thought captive to obey Christ.

—2 CORINTHIANS 10:5

In other words, the key to overcoming self-doubt is to go back to God's Word and get His vision. This applied to Joshua when he used the memory of God's words to improve his attitude so he could successfully face a huge logistical and military challenge. Similarly, writing the vision statement for my book enabled me to focus on completing this daunting task. Getting a new vision—God's vision—is the key to overcoming self-doubt in the sometimes challenging season of singleness.

When we read God's Word and meditate on it day and night, we adopt His vision, which gives us confidence. When we focus on God, something happens inside our hearts: He works His miracles, changes our negative thoughts to positive ones, and provides us with the confidence we need.

Confidence Lesson #3: Replace Fear with Faith

The antidote to fear is faith. No other cure is needed. All we have to do is to tell fear to leave and that it has no place in our lives. The

Bible contains 365 passages telling us, "Do not fear." God knows that fear is a massive challenge for us, so in His love, He provided us with one reassurance for every day of the year.

The Bible also contains many stories that illustrate the fact that faith overcomes fear. For example, in his gospel, Mark relates the following story of the disciples relying on their faith when crossing a stormy lake (Mark 4:35-41).

One night, Jesus and his disciples decided to cross Lake Gennesaret in a small boat. As they set out, the green reeds at the shore were swaying in a gentle breeze. But by the time they were in the middle of the lake, a storm arose, and large waves crashed over the bow of their boat. "We're going to die!" they screamed. "Help! Help!" Jesus had fallen asleep, so the disciples were afraid He was unaware of their dire situation.

That is how I sometimes feel when confronted with the challenges of singleness. I'm in the middle of a fear storm, panicked with the thought that I'm all alone, and thinking that God is miles away from me and isn't going to help me.

On Lake Gennesaret, why was Jesus sleeping while his disciples fought for their survival? Because He had faith, knowing neither the waves nor the wind would put them in any danger and that everything was under God's control. Could that be a reason that we do not always feel Him close to us, and it seems as if He's not doing anything? We see the immediate threat and are fearful, even though God is calm and knows everything will turn out as it should in the end. That is hard for us to believe sometimes. Rather than relying on our faith to combat our fears, we want to feel God's presence and to see Him intervene more often.

When the disciples did finally wake up Jesus in the boat, He brought relief:

> *He got up, rebuked the wind and said to the waves, "Quiet! Be still!" Then the wind died down, and it was completely calm.*
>
> **—MARK 4:39 (NIV)**

And here comes the killer: After that, he rebuked his disciples, saying:

> *"Why are you so afraid? Have you still no faith?"*
>
> **—MARK 4:40**

Right there, He tells us that the sure cure for fear is faith: faith in a God who is stronger than any challenge or any problem we may face, greater than any disease, and bigger than anything we lack. When we believe, our insecurity vanishes.

If you fear being alone, God says, "I am with you."

If you are afraid of missing out, God says, "I will provide."

If you fear God cannot handle a problem, He says, "I have everything under control."

If you are afraid of being lost or trapped, God says, "I am the way."

If you are frightened of the possibility of being single all your life, God tells you, "I will give you an abundant life in every season of your life."

If you fear you will not recognize the right moment to meet your soulmate, God says, "I will instruct you and teach you in the way you should go."

If you fear God has left you, He says, "I am with you, in the boat—and always."

Confidence Lesson #4: Exercise to Elevate Your Mood

As strange as it may sound, I found physical exercise to help overcome self-doubt. The day I felt so depressed and did not appreciate the beautiful sunrise was on one of my gym workout days, which meant I did not do my usual cardio workout. However, the next day I woke up early and went running. Afterward, when I looked in the mirror, I saw a different guy. Whereas the day before, I was full of doubts and insecurities, after my run I felt stronger, happier, more secure, more confident, and more optimistic about my future.

Humans are made up of three parts—spirit, mind, and body—and the three work together. So, it makes sense if we nurture our body through physical exercise, we will also elevate our spirit and mind. I find that exercise puts me into a new state in which I am ready to take action. In chemistry class, I learned the concept of activation energy: Once energy passes a threshold, a chemical reaction will start and continue to the very end. It's like a ball pushed to the top of the hill that rolls on its own down the slope on the other side. Likewise, physical exertion activates our mind and spirit and propels us to accomplish things.

Exercising also facilitates positive thinking. When I feel good after exercising, I find I'm much more optimistic. And once I begin to feel optimistic, it's more difficult for me to be depressed. Have you ever held a rotating bicycle wheel in your hands and tried to pivot the axle? It takes a lot of energy. Why? Because there is momentum. Physical exercise creates a feel-good momentum in me that steers me toward optimism and away from pessimism and depression. In other words, exercise helps me feel more confident.

Confidence Lesson #5: Seek Out Good Role Models

In my life, I find it valuable to know other long-term single people and also those who were single for a long time and are now married. With both groups, I learn from their struggles and grow in confidence knowing they have gone through challenges similar to mine and have emerged from them triumphant and thriving. Also, I find both sets of friends to be excellent resources to answer my many questions about singleness.

Mike Pilavachi, one of the few pastors I've heard of who is single, inspires me. I find his confidence and willingness to share his experiences in his own, very humorous, way make him an ideal role model for single people like me. In a television interview, Mr. Pilavachi said, "My Mom wanted me to have a girlfriend and sex already when I was a teenager. But I refused. Until this day I have not had sex with any living creature, nor any vegetable either!" I loved his honesty. He was not ashamed of not having a girlfriend, because he realized his purpose in his single season.

What a privilege it is to have such wonderful role models to look up to. I would not be where I am now if it were not for the excellent examples set by other long-term singles and former singles who are now married. Perhaps God may use you or me to encourage other single people He places in our lives. By becoming role models for others, we also would gain confidence, thriving in the knowledge that we helped others.

CHAPTER 4: WRAP-UP

Realizing fear was paralyzing me led me to look for ways to gain confidence. I first had to conquer the fear that caused me to doubt myself and feel insecure. By reading His Word, God helped me understand that He believed in me. With this knowledge, I was able to intentionally throw out my negative thoughts and replace fear with faith in God, who is greater and more powerful than any challenge we may encounter. Surprisingly, I discovered that physical exercise enabled this change by elevating my mood. And last, but not least, I turned to other long-term single people, and gained new confidence from them, knowing they also experienced challenges and, despite them, were able to find confidence.

CHAPTER 4: TAKEAWAYS

DISPELLING FEARS AND FINDING CONFIDENCE

POINTS TO CONSIDER

1. Various fears about your marital status may weigh heavily on your mind and make you feel insecure and doubt yourself.

2. To conquer these fears, identify and examine each one individually. If you put your trust in God and let Him handle your situation, He will change your heart and, as a result, you will gain confidence.

3. Gaining confidence is a process. While God is doing His part of changing you, you can contribute to your transformation by realizing God believes in you, modifying your negative thoughts, replacing fear with faith, doing physical exercise to elevate your mood, and seeking out good role models.

QUESTIONS FOR GROUPS

1. What are your biggest fears about being single?

2. What is your biggest roadblock hindering you from finding confidence?

ACTION STEPS TO TAKE

1.   Read and reflect on Joshua 1:1-9 (NIV):

After the death of Moses, the servant of the Lord, the Lord said to Joshua, son of Nun, Moses' aide: "Moses my servant is dead. Now then, you and all these people, get ready to give to them—to the Israelites. I will give you every place where you set your foot, as I promised Moses. Your territory will extend from the desert to Lebanon, and from the great river, the Euphrates—all the Hittite country—to the Mediterranean Sea in the west. No one will be able to stand against you all the days of your life. As I was with Moses, so I will be with you; I will never leave you nor forsake you. Be strong and courageous, because you will lead these people to inherit the land I swore to their ancestors to give them.

"Be strong and very courageous. Be careful to obey all the laws my servant Moses gave you; do not turn from it to the right or to the left, that you may be successful wherever you go. Keep this Book of the Law always on your lips; meditate on

it day and night, so that you may be careful to do
everything written in it. Then you will be prosperous
and successful. Have I not commanded you? Be
strong and courageous. Do not be afraid; do not be
discouraged, for the Lord your God will be with you
wherever you go."

2. Remember charismatic author and speaker Joyce Meyer's quote: "When fear knocks on your door, send faith to answer." Consider its meaning in your life.

CHAPTER 5

HEALING THE WOUNDS OF PAST RELATIONSHIPS

God's breath is like a fresh wind that renews us.
Frail and weak as we are, we have hope.
We find healing.

—JHIESS KRIEG, INSPIRATIONAL AUTHOR

STORY OF A SINGLE

My marriage was difficult. At one point, I realized I had to let go of my life and put everything into the hands of God. I had no choice. Even though my former husband and I tried everything we could think of to save our marriage, eventually we came to the point where we called it quits.

Divorce had never been part of my plans, and yet I felt God managing this season of my life, too. He gave me the ability to stop being angry with my ex. Forgiving him was challenging. Nevertheless, I chose to forgive him anyway. After our marriage ended, I had no regrets because I felt I had given everything I could possibly give to the relationship. Even though I didn't feel guilty, I was heartbroken because I lost the man I loved.

I couldn't have gone through the divorce alone. I got help immediately, reaching out to God and many good friends who helped me undergo my long and painful process of restoration. In the beginning, I spent most of my days on my couch, watching TV. At that stage, I let God do all the work.

In the middle of my healing process, I met a guy who was interested in me. After talking for a while, I found myself falling into the same unhealthy patterns as I had with my ex-husband. "Why do I keep running into the same kind of person?" I asked.

My counselor explained, "In your mind, you have unconscious hooks you can't see that attach to other people's hooks. Your hooks are positioned in such a way they attract people with matching hooks. Imagine getting rid of your current set of hooks, though, and letting God give you new ones, ones that will attract men better suited to your needs."

One day, God revealed to me that I had been living in survival mode for too long. My life seemed like a cold, dark place filled with fear that kept me from moving forward. God said, "From now on, you must choose to live." I was scared but responded, "Okay, Lord. I trust you. I'll do whatever You put in front of me. My life is in Your hands." I cried a lot because of the overwhelming challenge: I had to let go of my fear of living, of falling back into past emotions, and of perhaps getting new wounds. Countless times I proclaimed, "You're in charge, God, because I can't handle this." I allowed Him to heal my heart. When I took Communion, I visualized the blood Jesus shed for my sufferings, and saw it enter into all the cracks in my heart and seal those wounds.

I compared my condition to having two broken legs. You have to spend the first days in bed since you can't do anything else other than wait to get better. Then you move on to a wheelchair, and finally, you have to learn to walk again—first with crutches and then without. It meant a lot of hard work for me.

During the entire process of healing from my divorce, I would often praise God, telling Him He was the King of Kings. No matter what I was going through, I learned when I was weak that He merited my praise because He is wonderful and doesn't change. I put all my trust in God and told Him, "I don't want to find a new soulmate for myself. I want to accept the one You have in store for me." I decided not to make a list of requirements for a spouse because I didn't want to influence God. I wanted Him to choose the right man for me. He knows what I care about and like. But I have to admit that I have a few silly little wishes: I want him to have beautiful hair and a nice look.

Looking back, I see God knows what He's doing. He restored me. I found an abundant life again, and to my surprise, God led a wonderful new man into my life who exceeds my expectations.

—CHRYSTEL, THIRTY-TWO YEARS OLD, SWITZERLAND

Chances are, if you're like me, you have been involved in at least one unsuccessful romantic relationship. Perhaps you only went on one or two dates before you decided to call it quits. Or maybe you participated in a serious relationship—or two or three of them—that lasted a long time. If you broke up after saying, "Until death shall part us," you have a legal document—a divorce decree—that reminds you of your failure to sustain your relationship. When I lived in the French-speaking part of Switzerland, every time I had to declare my relationship status, I was reminded of my failure: the French word *célibataire*, which means "single," looks very similar to the English word "celibacy," that state of eternal singleness I wanted to avoid.

Failure is part of our lives and is how we learn. However, we don't like to fail because it's hard, and it hurts. When it comes to relationships that are full of emotional entanglements, failure is much harder, and the wounds of those failures need time to heal.

I have been involved in several romantic relationships in my life. So far, all of them have been unsuccessful, in that none of them have led to marriage. Every single time I come out of a relationship, I feel like a failure; I assume the breakup was primarily my fault, and I search diligently for the mistakes I made. That is my personality. But over time, I've come to reevaluate these failed relationships to learn from them: to grow and to change, so that I will be more successful in my next one.

MY FIRST SERIOUS RELATIONSHIP

At a church camp near the Mediterranean Sea, instead of concentrating on my beach volleyball game, I kept looking at a girl wearing fashion sunglasses, sitting on the near side of the field. To me, the game had become no more than a ploy to get closer to that beautiful girl. I hoped she was looking at me, too. Her sun-tanned skin made it difficult to guess whether she was Swiss or Spanish, but I didn't care. I was fascinated by her and wanted to get to know her. Even though we belonged to the same church, we did not know each other.

The next day when I witnessed Lauren's incredible creativity in a camp art class, I fell in love with her. I smelled roses everywhere we went: roses here, roses there, roses everywhere. I was twenty-nine years old and hoped a relationship with Lauren might enable me to achieve my life-long dream of being married by the time I was thirty.

Unfortunately, our relationship, which began so well, didn't progress the way I hoped. The roses seemed to stay at the beautiful Mediterranean beach. When we got back home to Switzerland, my attraction for Lauren soon waned, and I was no longer in love with her. I convinced myself I was just suffering from post-vacation blues, and so we continued to date, but after a month, I realized I felt trapped in our relationship and thought about ending it, but was afraid of hurting Lauren by breaking up with her after such a short time. And I was wary of what my friends would say now that they had accepted Lauren as my girlfriend. "Isn't a dating relationship supposed to be difficult at times?" I reasoned. That's what my married friends had told me. Besides, I wasn't a guy who gave up easily.

I continued dating Lauren, thinking that things would improve. Since it was my first serious relationship, I did not realize that her intense mood swings might indicate emotional problems. I didn't know how to handle such an unhealthy relationship, but I kept trying because I wanted it to work. In hindsight and with regret, I must say I pushed it way too far because of the fear of failure and ridicule. After ten months, I finally summed up the courage to call it quits.

The failure of my first serious dating relationship tore me apart, causing me to become pessimistic and then depressed. My parents, who had never seen me like that, told me they were worried about my emotional state. Fortunately, God held his protecting hand over me and guided me through my three-year healing process.

> *Rejoice not over me, O my enemy;*
> *when I fall, I shall rise.*
>
> **—MICAH 7:8**

Like the prophet Micah, I resolved to rise again—to date other women—and so decided to see a counselor. For my friends, this came as a surprise. I belonged to a group of men who had a low opinion of counseling, saying things like, "Why would I ever do such a thing? That's not for me, only for girls and those who have some serious issues." Now I see how short-sighted our views were.

Today I am a big fan of counseling because it has been a substantial part of my emotional healing process and has helped me become a better person. I am so grateful for the counselors, both professionals and caring friends, who have walked beside me, taught me much, and helped me heal. I would never be where I am at today without them.

Counseling enabled me to process my relationship with Lauren and learn from it. And the lessons I learned made me stronger than before. Although our relationship was unsuccessful in that we didn't end up getting married, I do not view it as a failure. In my eyes, failure only occurs when we don't try our hardest and just play it safe. If we take courage, fix the broken things, and learn from our past experiences, we succeed. I like this verse from Proverbs:

> *The godly may trip seven times, but they will get up again.*
>
> **—PROVERBS 24:16 (NLT)**

So, if an unsuccessful relationship has caused you to trip and fall, don't stay down. Get up, fix whatever broke, and then move forward. Never play it safe. Get off your couch and go find the roses.

GOD HEALS A HARDENED HEART

Your past relationships and prolonged times of singleness may result in a hardened heart: one not willing to take the chance of falling in love and possibly being hurt again. You are not the first one to have a hardened heart; many have been there before. Fortunately for all of us, God knows how to heal this problem:

And I will give you a new heart, and a new spirit I will put within you. And I will remove the heart of stone from your flesh and give you a heart of flesh.

—EZEKIEL 36:26

Many experiences may lead to a hardened heart. For me, these experiences include: attending a wedding as the only single person there; hearing a friend say, "You're weird," just because I'm unmarried; going through a breakup; and enduring long periods of loneliness. If I'm not careful, situations like these may cause me to have a hardened heart.

> *When I sit in darkness, the Lord will*
> *be a light to me.*
>
> —MICAH 7:8

What moments of darkness have you experienced in your life? What did those moments do to your heart? Consider putting this book aside for a minute and writing about these experiences.

After my split with Lauren, I had a hardened heart and didn't know what to do about it. Counseling helped me understand why the relationship was unsuccessful, but it left me feeling disappointed and wounded. I was afraid of repeating my mistakes and frightened of being hurt again. In short, my heart was hardened. And then, through prayer and patience, God changed me. Even if I did not see it, I felt Him working. But it was not an overnight quick-fix. My emotional healing took many years, during which He gradually replaced my heart of stone with a new heart: tender, soft, patient, and ready to love again.

As God was fixing my heart, I believe He provided me with a temporary layer of armor. He knew I was vulnerable and wanted to protect me until I was ready to deal with a relationship again. As I regained my full strength, this extra protection gradually disappeared, as if He told me, "You have enough strength now; you can handle whatever life throws at you." This reassures me that He is a caring Father.

He protects and empowers us, giving us just what we need exactly when we need it.

What God did for me, He also can do for you, because miracles happen when God is at work. Does your heart need repair? Are you ready to let Him transform you, too?

OVERCOMING SELF-PITY

The post-breakup period of a relationship may be dangerous. If we do not find the courage to stand up, dust ourselves off, and try again, we may go down the seductive road of self-pity. Why is this road so attractive? Because it's easy. Getting up is hard. Like when my alarm clock wakes me in the morning—it is very easy to hit the snooze button and stay in bed. Getting up takes much more willpower and energy.

I like the definition of "self-pity" found in the Merriam-Webster dictionary: "a self-indulgent dwelling on one's sorrows or misfortunes." It allows for the fact that we all have difficulties in our lives, calling them "sorrows or misfortunes," but cautions against paying too much attention to them by referring to such excessive attention as a "self-indulgent dwelling," a phrase full of negative connotations.

After a breakup, a certain amount of self-pity is natural and part of the healing process. To recover from any injury, we must examine our wounds and tend to them. But if we're not careful, this examination may trap us into a feeling of victimhood. Self-pity resembles a weed: if you are not mindful of it when it first appears, the unwanted plant will soon overtake the entire garden.

If you want to overcome self-pity, you first must learn to recognize it and decide to do something about it. In Chapter 4, we discussed how we are not victims of our thoughts, but can actively manipulate them to serve our purposes, focusing on the positive rather than the negative. I find the same to be true about self-pity. Once I identify its existence in my life, I work hard to redirect its negative thoughts into positive ones and find worship and prayer to be the most useful tools to accomplish this. When I focus on God's goodness, my perspective pivots, my outlook on life improves, and my self-pity vanishes.

FORGIVENESS

Your healing process begins when you FORGIVE those who have wronged you, LOVE those who hate you, and PRAY for those who prey on you.

—UNKNOWN

I found that to complete the healing process after a breakup, I had to forgive my ex, which I did. To my surprise, though, I realized forgiving myself was a key ingredient, as well. If I could not forgive myself for all wrongs, my healing would not be complete. I was surprised to find forgiving myself was much harder than forgiving others. In particular, it was hard to feel this self-forgiveness in my heart. I knew I had to do it—my mind was ready to forgive—yet my heart struggled. I had carried the burden of failure for so long, I found it difficult to release. I had to be patient and allow time for my heart to believe that God forgave me everything. Once I did that, I could fully heal. David describes it in a Psalm:

Blessed is the one whose transgression is forgiven, whose sin is covered. Blessed is the man against whom the Lord counts no iniquity, and in whose spirit there is no deceit.

—PSALM 32:1-2

Forgiveness starts with the knowledge God forgives. If you repent, God will forgive you. He promised it:

You will cast all our sins into the depths of the sea.

—MICAH 7:19

When God forgives us, He forgets all about our sins by casting them far away. Which sin? "All our sins." That includes every wrong we have ever done, without exception or size limit. God throws them "into the depths of the sea" and completely forgives us for them. And yet, I often did not forgive myself but continued to carry the weight of my past mistakes. How ridiculous. Why should I do such a thing when God Himself has forgiven me?

Many centuries later, Paul comments again on God's forgiveness, reminding us of this liberating truth:

There is therefore now no condemnation for those who are in Christ Jesus.

—ROMANS 8:1

In that passage, the small, two-letter word "no" changes everything. There is "no condemnation" because Jesus has forgiven us.

The Bible makes it clear: David said God forgives all our sins, and Paul built on this idea. God does not point His finger at us, putting us down for our mistakes and failures. He wants to uplift us and restore our souls. The enemy is the one who tries to push us down. He knows that we are God's children and that he cannot snatch us from God's hand. The enemy wants us to believe that we are still flawed.

The French language helped me understand the importance of forgiveness. If someone has done me wrong, in French, I say, "*Je lui en veux.*" The figurative translation is, "I am holding a grudge against him," but it literally means, "I want what he has." In other words, someone has taken something from me that I am now lacking, and he won't give it back to me. The only thing I can do is to imagine myself freely offering that thing to him as if I had decided to give it to him in the first place. (Please bear with me; I know this is a thought exercise.) If I think of the giving as being my idea—not his—forgiveness can take place. And that is what I needed to do for me to forgive myself. Otherwise, I would remain miserable. In the words of David:

> *For when I kept silent, my bones wasted away through my groaning all day long.*
>
> **—PSALM 32:3**

God wants to make us whole again. If you feel there is someone you have not forgiven, put this book aside, and forgive the person who hurt you. If you feel you have already forgiven, reflect on your forgiveness. Have you forgiven completely? Or is there any specific transgression you are still holding against someone else or yourself? If so, you may want to use this prayer to let God know you want to forgive everyone completely—including yourself—and that you need His help:

Dear Lord,

I thank You for the power of forgiveness, and I choose to forgive everyone who has hurt me. Help me set [name anyone who has offended you] free and release them to You [Romans 12:19]. Help me bless those who have hurt me [Romans 12:14]. Help me walk in righteousness, peace, and joy, demonstrating Your life here on earth. I choose to be kind and compassionate, forgiving others, just as You forgave me [Ephesians 4:32].

In Jesus's name, amen.

—DEBBIE PRZYBYLSKI, FOUNDER OF INTERCESSORS ARISE INTERNATIONAL

GOD IS GOOD

If you doubt God is good, He will prove it to you, over and over again. This is another critical step of your healing: Remember that God is good to you—and everyone—all the time. His Word gives me confidence that He is watching over me and that He protects me.

You are a hiding place for me; you preserve me from trouble.

—PSALM 32:7

Bless the Lord, O my soul, and all that is within me, bless his holy name! Bless the Lord, O my soul, and forget not all his benefits, who forgives all your iniquity, who heals all your diseases, who redeems your life from the pit, who crowns you with steadfast love and mercy, who satisfies you with good so that your youth is renewed like the eagle's.

—PSALM 103:1-5

ANOTHER UNSUCCESSFUL RELATIONSHIP

When I first met the woman I will call Jennifer, I thought a relationship with her would be a piece of cake. She seemed to embrace many of the same core values I considered essential and was active in the church, leading a small group and participating in counselor training. Based on my initial impressions, Jennifer seemed like an ideal candidate to become my soulmate.

At first, she didn't seem very enthusiastic about dating me, but I thought once she got to know me better, she'd become more interested. Throughout the spring and early summer, I called her often, and we went out on occasional dates. However, her enthusiasm for me did not seem to grow, so that mid-summer, when some friends of mine became involved in the renovation of a cinema to become our new church, I decided to break off my relationship with Jennifer so I could participate in that exciting project. When I went to tell her this, though, she told me she'd decided she finally did want to date me more seriously. Since I had been pursuing her for months, I reluctantly passed up the chance to work on the church project and committed myself to explore a committed relationship with her.

Our relationship quickly became quite physical, even though that made me uncomfortable. Despite Jennifer's objections, I insisted we not sleep in the same room, and definitely not in the same bed. We often fought about our different expectations of our physical relationship. Then we began fighting about other things, too: politics, different views of our faith, even the correct way to take Communion. She seemed to enjoy our verbal sparring matches, but I found them exhausting and became unhappy in our relationship. As we continued to see each other, the friction between us grew. Finally, she let me know she wanted to continue to live in the same city where she currently resided. I, on the other hand, wanted to explore the world and was dreaming of living abroad somewhere, learning another language, and discovering a new culture. For me, this was the deal-breaker, and I called off the relationship soon after. Jennifer was shocked and hurt and wrote me a scathing letter detailing how I had wronged her. To make matters worse, her best friend, who was also a good friend of mine, refused to talk to me ever again. I had hoped that Jennifer and I could part ways amicably, but that was not possible.

And now, I had to deal with yet another failure. I felt devastated. Why couldn't I make a relationship work? Once again, it took me a long time to recover. During this process, I found encouragement in many different places. For example, during a counseling training session, an instructor spoke to me about relationships, even though he had no idea what I was going through. He said everyone needs a spouse with compatible spiritual goals. If your desires diverge too much, your relationship will not work. Wow. I felt like his words validated my decision to break up with Jennifer. The instructor later became my counselor.

Due to the good advice I received from that instructor and other sources, I knew I had done the right thing and found hope in knowing that better days would come. However, just like the ending of my first relationship, my road to recovery was no smooth ride. Feelings of guilt kept coming back. Once again, I had to not only forgive my ex but also myself, too. I found prayers like this one to be helpful:

Compassionate Father,

Thank you for forgiving me and giving me the gift of abundant, eternal life. You are the God who blots out my transgressions and remembers my sins no more. When I am reminded of my past failures, free me from despair and shame. My debt has been completely paid by Jesus. I am free from condemnation, free from guilt, and free from shame. Let me be transformed into your likeness through the presence of your Holy Spirit living in me. Through Jesus Christ, our Lord. Amen.

—HTTPS://CONNECTUSFUND.ORG

As part of my recovery, I also had to learn to believe in myself again, but this was difficult. I thought everything was my fault and that I had made Jennifer a victim of my cruel breakup. Once again, I turned to counseling for help to see through those lies and find a healthier self-concept. I came to understand I had made mistakes, but she had failed too since when a relationship doesn't work, it is usually the result of failures of both parties. I was not a bad person just because our relationship had failed.

God healed my heart and helped me to understand what I truly wanted. Now, I feel confident that someday I will be a good spouse and father. Not a perfect one, because nobody is, but one who is ready to grow, learn, take risks, and—when something does not work—say, "I'm sorry," and then change. And, like David, I pray to God for His guidance:

> *The troubles of my heart are enlarged; bring me out of my distress.*
>
> **—PSALM 25:17**

FINDING SUPPORT

When I was trying to heal from the wounds of past relationships, I found valuable support from four main sources: my friends, my parents, the Word of God, and counseling. Each of them contributed in a unique way to helping me stand up again and open my heart to love.

Support #1: Friends

My friends play a pivotal role in my life. They are the ones who accept me as I am; I know I can share my troubles with them, and they won't reject me. Because of that, my friends mean a lot to me. I am grateful for their encouragement, empathy, advice, and occasional kicks in the butt. They walk beside me when I go through "the valley of the shadow of death" (Psalm 23:4), and they never stop believing in me.

Support #2: My Parents

I am lucky to have a great relationship with my parents, who are still a vital source of support for me. Their words of wisdom and knowledge help me see the big picture in situations so I can make the right decisions. They give me the freedom to make my own choices, never telling me what to do. Instead, they assist and advise me in my decision-making process as a counselor would do.

Support #3: The Word of God: The Best Support

I draw a considerable amount of wisdom from God's Word. For *Single for a Season*, I've included personal stories from my life, the lives of friends, as well as many passages from the Bible. Because the Word of God has power and gives us the insight we need to move forward in life.

> *I will instruct you and teach you in the way you should go; I will counsel you with my eye upon you.*
>
> **—PSALM 32:8**

God's Word comes alive if we take the time to read it and meditate on it. It gives us understanding. There is no higher source of wisdom. Let us take full advantage of what is at our disposal. After all, the Bible is a precious collection of the world's best inspirational writers.

Support #4: Counseling

Last but not least, my counselors have helped me undergo profound self-reflection. I would not be the person I am today if I had not spent many hours with them, sharing my experiences and answering their thought-provoking questions. Counseling accelerated my inner healing and helped me in two major ways: rationally and emotionally.

As a person with a scientific background, I found counseling appealed to my logical nature. Gaining more knowledge and understanding of my character and personality through counseling helped me realize why I reacted to different situations in certain ways. Also, I became aware of what I needed to watch out for in the future. I call this the rational part of the support I gained from my counseling.

Counselors also helped me understand my emotions. Their numerous, probing questions forced me to dig deep into my heart for answers and prompted hidden feelings to surface. Because of this, I became more focused on forgiving others and myself. Knowing the underlying reasons for my issues enabled me to pray for my specific needs instead of making general and superficial requests.

CHAPTER 5: WRAP-UP

In conclusion, we have all participated in unsuccessful relationships, but we shouldn't see these as failures. Failure is allowing our mistakes to knock us down and lose hope. Instead, I invite you to get back up again after an unsuccessful relationship and experience healing change. Leadership coach Robin Sharma wrote, "All change is hard at first, messy in the middle, and it's gorgeous at the end." At the end of the sometimes painful healing process, you will arrive at the beautiful, peaceful place David described:

You prepare a table before me in the presence of my enemies; you anoint my head with oil; my cup overflows.

Surely goodness and mercy shall follow me all the days of my life, and I shall dwell in the house of the Lord forever.

—PSALM 23:5-6

CHAPTER 5: TAKEAWAYS

HEALING THE WOUNDS OF PAST RELATIONSHIPS

POINTS TO CONSIDER

1. Falling down and failing is not your biggest concern. Staying down is. See failure as a learning opportunity. Get up, fix whatever broke, forgive whoever wronged you, forgive yourself, and then move forward.

2. Emotional pain due to bad experiences, unsuccessful relationships, self-pity, or prolonged periods of singleness may harden your heart. But God, through His supernatural touch, is capable of softening and healing your heart if you let Him do His work.

3. Instead of feeling sorry for yourself, reach out for help. Telling your friends, family, a professional relationship coach, or a counselor that you need their support is the first step to a healing change.

QUESTIONS FOR GROUPS

1. What was your biggest breakup challenge? How did you overcome it?

2. What have you learned from unsuccessful relationships? Share what you would do the same versus what you would do differently the next time.

ACTION STEPS TO TAKE

1. Contact a friend or counselor today.

2. Ask them to help you heal your emotional wounds, forgive yourself, and forgive whoever may have hurt you.

CHAPTER 6

BECOMING WHOLE

I'm happy as I am, and love my liberty too well to be in a hurry to give it up for any mortal man.

—FROM GOOD WIVES BY LOUISA MAY ALCOTT

STORY OF A SINGLE

I enjoy my single season, particularly my freedom. I don't feel I need someone to be with me—perhaps in the future.

A few weeks ago, one of my cousins asked me, "Why didn't you get married?"

I replied, "Please don't ask me about my marital status. It's not important."
I said this not because I wanted to avoid the topic or because I couldn't stand being alone, but because I don't feel lonely since my identity in God makes me confident. I

refuse to let others pressure me to get married. God is my provider. In Him, I can find everything I need. Neither material things nor a boyfriend can fulfill me. That's why I look up to God.

After I graduated high school, I did feel lonely because everyone around me was in a relationship. It annoyed me that my parents and my family said that I should get married. They knew that many guys were interested in me. The influence of the people around me led me to think that I should date someone. But when I did date, I realized that a relationship couldn't fill my void.

Later, the more I studied God's Word, the more I based my identity on being with Him. Drawing closer to Him, I laid my future into His hands and heard Him urge me to live my life to its fullest. Today, I encourage others to do the same by saying, "Be who you are, don't be fake, don't imitate anyone else." That's the way I live; I am who I am.

One of my friends recently asked me, "Why don't you want a boyfriend or a husband?"

I replied, "Jesus is my everything."

She didn't like my answer, but it was the truth: His presence fills me. It wouldn't be hard for me to date someone, but deep inside, I feel that I don't want it now.

Two guys—who I didn't know at all—asked my parents if they could marry me. Each time, my parents asked me, "Do you want to take him as your husband?"

"Absolutely not! I'll marry the guy I choose," I said. "I respect you and I'm thankful to have you as my parents, but everybody should be able to decide who to marry."

Another time a good friend asked me if I wanted to be his wife. Although he was cute and smart, I did not feel that this was the love I wanted.

There's no need for me to have a guy to fulfill me since God meets my needs. I believe all we have to do is to trust in God. Whenever the right time comes, He will show me the right person for my life. I stay positive and calm, knowing He is our provider.

—SOPHEAP, THIRTY-ONE YEARS OLD, CAMBODIA

WAYS TO FIND WHOLENESS IN THE SINGLE SEASON

My life plan to get married before I turned thirty did not work out. As I approached my forties, I began to reflect on my life as a single person. "Who am I? What should I do? Who does God want me to be?" Until then, I had not given much consideration to staying single since that had never been my intention.

What identity do we have as single women and men? What does the Bible say about us? Do we have a specific purpose? Does our identity depend on whether we are married? In this chapter, we're going to explore our identity as singles and look at ways we can be whole.

Method #1: See the Single Season as a Gift of Time to Become a Better You

I found David's story in 1 Samuel 16 helped me find many answers. Once the prophet Samuel had anointed David as the new King of Israel, the young shepherd went back to tend his sheep for another twenty years. Why did God allow such a long waiting period? I think David needed first to understand who he was. Becoming king is no easy task. The danger is that you become proud, unbalanced, tyrannical, and self-centered. On the day of his anointing, the young shepherd boy was not ready to lead the Israelites. To become a good king, David had to become whole first.

Likewise, because we are single, we get a unique opportunity to develop our identity in Christ now. I am not saying that we are not ready for a relationship. Maybe yes, maybe no. Either way, this time can be an opportunity to grow as a woman or a man of God. In this single season, if we allow Him, God will complete us. To quote Paul, "[The

133

Lord] said, 'My grace is all you need'" (2 Corinthians 12:9 [NLT]).

Author, blogger, and media specialist, Rania Naim, published a blog article entitled, "The Happiest People Are Those Who Realized That God Is Enough."[3] In it, she writes, "I want their faith. I want their strength. I want their solid feet when their world is falling apart. I want their forgiveness when their heart is breaking. I want their pace in moving on when something isn't meant to be. I want their ease in letting go of what they can't control. I want their peace of mind, knowing that God is enough, knowing that God is writing their story, knowing that God has better things planned for them, and knowing that loving God is the only love they really need in their lives." I like the conclusions she drew: "People find happiness when they find God. People understand life, when they understand God. People truly start living when they make God their guide, their leader, and their voice."

If we know Christ completes us, we receive a supernatural peace. When we understand that God is enough, our lives pivot, and our perspective changes. In Ms. Naim's words, "Once you learn that God is enough, you'll never have to question yourself, you'll never have to doubt yourself or your decisions. You become whole again. You become complete."

One very beneficial side-effect of this is that you begin to change your criteria for your future spouse. As you feel complete, you no longer believe you need to find someone who completes you. This person does not exist, anyway. Instead, you begin to look for a spouse who *complements* you. That's a game-changer. You see yourself as a gift rather than as a person lacking something.

---

3 Rania Naim, "The Happiest People Are Those Who Realized That God Is Enough," Thought Catalog, last modified December 27, 2020, https://thoughtcatalog.com/rania-naim/2017/05/the-happiest-people-are-those-who-realized-that-god-is-enough/.

As I was speaking to Annie, a woman you will read more about in Chapter 7, she told me, "As a young adult, I read a quote by Dr. Myles Munroe that resonated with me. He said, 'Singleness is wholeness.' Before that time, I never identified myself as a single person; I thought of myself as God's daughter. I first needed to know who I was. Only then, I was ready to meet my husband and build a solid relationship."

By the day David finally did assume the role of king, he had become another person: mature and wise. He wasn't perfect and made significant mistakes during his reign, but God called him a man after His heart. I dream of a generation of single men and women after God's heart. Are you willing to embrace the opportunity God gives you in the single season—and to use it to love God more? David needed additional time to become grounded in God's identity. If your values do not stem from your identity in God, you will get sidetracked. So, see the single season as a gift of time to become a better version of yourself.

Method #2: Focus on Your Relationships with Jesus

As I was writing this book, I asked my friend, Sarah, "What points do you focus on as a single person?"

She said, "I find the most essential focus in this season of my life is growing in my relationship with Jesus. I let Him transform my heart so I can give Him my entire heart." She explained to me that she wanted to fall in love with Jesus without expecting anything in return. "It's a big challenge," she said. "It's up to me to give everything to Him. He has already given everything to me."

> *And let us run with perseverance the race marked out for us, fixing our eyes on Jesus, the pioneer and perfecter of faith.*
>
> **—HEBREWS 12:1-2 (NIV)**

When we "fix our eyes on Jesus," we focus on Him and steer toward him because we tend to move toward whatever we are looking at. Have you ever noticed that when you intently focus on a target when throwing a ball, the chances are higher that you'll hit it? You fix your eyes on the target and the ball follows. Paulo Coelho wrote, "Whenever you want to achieve something, keep your eyes open, concentrate, and make sure know exactly what it is you want. No one can hit their target with their eyes closed." The writer of Hebrews knew this truth. He wanted Christians to become more Christ-like, which is God's dream for us, but realized it was a matter of focus. For us to be more like God, we first must concentrate our attention on Him.

Amidst the COVID pandemic, the Swiss light artist, Gerry Hofstetter, projected "#hope" over the red and white colors of the Swiss flag on the iconic 4,478-meter-high Matterhorn Mountain. He wanted the Swiss to look up and say, "There is still hope." It reminded me of Psalm 121:

I lift up my eyes to the mountains—where does my help come from? My help comes from the Lord, the Maker of heaven and earth.

—PSALM 121:1-2 (NIV)

Here we find the same concept again. Lift your eyes and focus on the Lord. Our help comes from Him, and other things, too. That is also where we find hope. There is a lot of hope in our singleness since God's promises still stand. To be able to run the race until the end, as Hebrews describes it, we need to keep looking at what is important: Jesus. And in turn, He fuels our hope.

I love dating, which is why I came up with the idea of going on dates with my King. Yes, that's right. I go on dates with Jesus. And the cool thing is they are fun. Spending time with Jesus fills my emotional tank. It touches my heart, makes me a new person, and helps me feel fulfilled. And that is when my inner void begins to disappear. Every moment I spend with Him, I become more whole. And I've found that Jesus always has time for me, and I can go out with Him as many times as I want.

I'm aware that a date with Jesus isn't the same as time spent with your future soulmate and may seem like a trivial theoretical exercise, but I encourage you to try it once. You will see how rewarding it is. Next time you are alone, instead of having a pity party, prepare dinner for two. Cook your favorite meal, set the table, light a candle, dim the lights, turn on great music, and serve dinner for you and Jesus. Imagine sitting with Him, looking into His eyes. Even though no one else is physically in your dining room, His presence will overflow your heart. I guarantee you it will be a life-changing experience. I hope you will join me in falling in love again with the King of the Universe.

There was a time when I did not feel my love for God. While searching for my soulmate, I lost my joy, and I didn't understand why God let me go through many tough relationships. Over time, my love for Him vanished. I didn't listen to Jesus when He wrote this message to the church in Philippi:

> *I know your works, your toil and your patient endurance, and how you cannot bear with those who are evil, but have tested those who call themselves apostles and are not, and found them to be false. I know you are enduring patiently and bearing up for my name's sake, and you have not grown weary. But I have this against you, that you have abandoned the love you had at first.*
>
> **—REVELATION 2:2-4**

By searching so hard for a relationship with a woman, I had lost my first love: my love for God. My prayer times and Bible studies grew stale as I did them with less passion. They had become something I had to do instead of something I wanted to do. Then, I took a one-month vacation. I had planned to travel to Australia, but listening to my soul, I decided to stay home. It was an unusual decision for me because I love to travel. But for those four weeks, I spent most of the time alone in my apartment, falling in love with Jesus again. I had many dates with Him, worshiping Him while sitting on my bed in my room, reading His Word, watching inspiring sermons, and listening to what He wanted me to hear. My smile grew bigger and bigger as I learned I preferred spending time with Him over going out to have drinks with friends. I needed to reconnect with God, and I did. By renewing my connection with God, I rediscovered a life to the fullest—life as good as it gets.

Method #3: Find Your Identity in Christ

When it comes to our identity in Christ, the word "single" is inconsequential. I am single, but my real identity does not stem from my singleness. First and foremost, I'm a child of God. And as we have seen before, in Christ, we are not alone. When we dwell in His presence, we discover our true identity.

The world we are living in focuses a lot on our relationship status. It's part of our Facebook profile. A plethora of commercials, music videos, and other social media sites tell us we should be in a relationship. Many documents and applications request information about your marital status. Thus, we are constantly reminded that we are single.

However, in Bible stories, whether the people are single or married is unimportant. For instance, the stories about Daniel do not mention anything about his relationship status. While a modern biographer dedicates much time to a celebrity's personal life, the Bible focuses on

Daniel's relationship with God. According to the Word, Daniel was a person rooted in God, dedicated to doing what He wanted him to do.

In a sermon I once heard, a pastor talked about what she learned while being single. "I discovered I had fewer opportunities to share what was on my heart with my friends. This forced me to develop the habit of speaking with God about things. And God is always ready to listen." Her experience inspired me to build my relationship with my Lord and Savior. Now that I have the habit of talking with Him first and have developed an intimate relationship with Jesus, I'm grateful for it.

Rather than looking for our identity in a relationship with another flawed human being or, even worse, in things like clothes, shoes, cars, or phones, we find our identity in Jesus. As we build our relationship with Him, He reveals who we are. Those revelations do not depend on trends or the ever-changing opinions of other people. What Jesus tells us is reliable and constant. We need to ground our identity in Christ. That's the only way of living.

One day I was given valuable insight into why becoming closer to Christ is so important. A friend drew a triangle on the board to explain what happens when you build a romantic relationship. He put the man and the woman at the two lower corners of the triangle, explaining there was a distance between them because of their different personalities, family histories, and perhaps values. God occupied the spot at the top of the triangle. Looking at us, my friend said, "When the man and woman move closer to Jesus, they both move upwards. As they move up, they also get closer to each other." In other words, by becoming closer to Christ, we get closer to each other in a relationship. And if we become closer to God now as a single person, we will be already closer to our future spouse when we meet him or her. That's the fantastic part of it.

I encourage you to make it a priority to become closer to Christ. It is something you have to plan. Spending time with Jesus will help you become a better person, and by devoting time to become closer with Him, you will find your identity in Christ.

Method #4: Search for Your Number Two

When asked why they want to be in a relationship, most people say they want to find someone to take care of and treasure. However, often those selfless words hide the truth: the relationship is more about me than my significant other. I want to fulfill my needs. I want to feel happy. I want to find a husband who will love me just as I am. I want a wife that gives me the confirmation I long for. Do these statements sound familiar? These desires are legitimate.

We need to look inside our hearts to understand why we truly want to be in a relationship. You have two options to choose from:

1. Look for Your Number One

"What type of woman am I looking for as a soulmate?" I wondered. Then, it dawned on me: I was searching for a woman who would complete me by filling in all of the places where I felt I was lacking, and by satisfying all of my desires. But no person can ever do all that, and if I continued to look for this perfect soulmate, I was sure to be disappointed. We want to find our Number One person who will make us feel complete, but before you start looking for such a person, understand there is a better way to handle it.

If Jesus becomes our Number One—the most important being in our life—we will be ready to date from a position of abundance instead of lack. Why? Because as Christ fills us up, we stop being desperate. He completes us, so we can refrain from looking for someone to fill all our voids. Before we start any dating relationship, we must change our social status to "in a relationship," because you and I are already in a relationship with our Number One: God, our first love.

2. Look for Your Number Two

Before he dated his future wife, one of my friends wore an engagement ring, signifying his commitment to his relationship with God. I liked the idea. Wearing a ring could help remind me that I'm in a relationship with God, which means that I'm whole right now, in this single season. I asked my friend if he was afraid the ring might scare off potential dates because they might think he was married. He said, "David, the women who take the time to get to know me will learn that I'm still single."

Once we have found our Number One, we are ready to search for our Number Two: our life partner. From our position of abundance, we can bestow this partner with gifts, because it's no longer about our needs, which are fulfilled by God. When I overflow because of my relationship with God, I am free to be a blessing for others, and I can give without asking anything in return.

Method #5: Run Your Race

A sermon by Pastor Carl Lentz gave me a new perspective on finding a soulmate. He encouraged us to focus on our ministry, on what God called us to. He said we can date and pursue a soulmate, but we should concentrate more on serving our Number One. After all, God promises when we seek His Kingdom first, He will take care of the rest. As Pastor Lentz said, "Serve. Get busy. After a while, lift your head, look to your left and your right. If you see your potential life partner, great! If not, keep serving. And then, after another while, look around again."

It reminded me of what my friend, Sarah, once told me: "Paul said you have to run your race. The person who will become our spouse will join us in this race and run beside us, moving forward with us and with God." Serving God and getting busy with what He lays on our hearts provides us with opportunities to align our desires with His. And it would be great to see someone special serving alongside us, and think, "Oh, wow! I'd like to get to know this person." As government policymaker, international trade advisor, and author Judith Hanna wrote, "Some of my closest friends have realized their best childhood friend, or that guy they volunteered alongside and never noticed, was the best dude for them." So, keep running your race. Do whatever God has called you to do. That is so much more valuable than browsing through countless dating profiles. And you might just find your soulmate running along beside you.

Sarah also said, "I have often questioned my identity because I was—and still am—single. Am I too much or too little like this or like that? Do I scare men away for some reason? As women, we question ourselves because we want to attract men. If no one pursues us, it may throw us off balance. I tend to look within myself to find what's wrong, what's scaring away the men. However, we must silence these types of lies. We don't need to please people of the opposite sex. Instead, please God, and the rest will follow." Run your race with God, and He will take care of the rest.

CHAPTER 6: WRAP-UP

There is good news: You and I are single people, and yet we are complete. We are never alone, we have a purpose, and we have a mission. Trust that everything is possible for Him.

I dream of becoming a husband who overflows and gives back to my wife rather than entering a relationship from a position of lack. How would you feel if you met a guy who wanted to date you because he thought he needed you to complete him? You could sense his first motivation was not a sincere love and interest in you but rather a selfish desire for his own happiness and fulfillment—even though he might not ever admit it.

If God completes me in Him, I will become more attractive, loving, caring, generous, and forgiving. This will benefit me when I build a dating relationship with the woman I fall in love with.

In the following verse, God calls David a man after His heart:

He raised up David to be their king, of whom he testified and said, 'I have found in David the son of Jesse a man after my heart, who will do all my will.'

—ACTS 13:22

David found his Number One: God, the Maker of the Universe. And he dedicated his life to following Him and obeying Him. Because of this devotion, David lacked nothing and said, "My cup overflows." David found his wholeness through spending time with God.

Likewise, becoming whole is the best way to become a good spouse for Mr. or Mrs. Betterhalf. If you find your Number One—your first love—in God, you will feel nothing is missing in you, not now in your singleness nor later when you find your Number Two—your soulmate—because Christ makes you whole.

CHAPTER 6: TAKEAWAYS
BECOMING WHOLE

POINTS TO CONSIDER

1. Seeing your season of singleness as a gift enables you to make the most out of your opportunity to grow as a woman or a man of God.

2. Your real identity stems from who you are in Christ—a child of the Most High—and not from your relationship status. When you ground your identity in Jesus, you understand that He is sufficient.

3. Realize Jesus is your Number One and make Him the most important person in your life. Doing so allows you to become whole and to date from a position of abundance instead of lack. That's when you are ready to search for your life partner: your Number Two.

QUESTIONS FOR GROUPS

1. How do you define your identity? Discuss this.

2. How have you experienced wholeness as a person while being single?

3.   In what ways are you still looking for someone to complete you, rather than seeking that completion from God?

ACTION STEPS TO TAKE

1.   Figure out the steps you need to take to become whole.

2.   Write them in your journal.

3.   Also, write a note to Jesus, telling Him you've decided to make Him your Number One.

CHAPTER 7

FINDING YOUR PURPOSE AS A SINGLE PERSON

Where there is no vision, the people perish.

—PROVERBS 29:18 (KJV)

The people who change the world are ordinary people with extraordinary ambition and dreams.

—BRIAN TRACY, MOTIVATIONAL SPEAKER AND AUTHOR

STORY OF A SINGLE

Most of my family and friends got married in their twenties. I felt irritated that some of them were putting pressure on me to do likewise. "When are you going to get married?" they would ask. I hated this question because it implied that as a woman, the main thing to aspire to and be defined by is finding the right person, settling down, and being a wife and a mother.

At a wedding, my aunt asked me, "So when is it going to be your turn?"

This question angered me to the extent that I publicly challenged her, replying, "Why are you asking me this rather than congratulating me on recently graduating with a master's degree. Do I have to have a partner to be fulfilled?"

I decided to embrace my single status, rather than succumbing to other people's expectations, and embraced the journey of singlehood. I began to accept that God's timing is perfect, and finding my identity and purpose in Christ became a higher priority.

When I was seventeen, I read In Pursuit of Purpose *by Dr. Myles Munroe. This book intrigued me and challenged me to find my God-given purpose and destiny through discovering my potential, gifts, and talents and maximizing them for the Kingdom. One quote in the book caught my attention: "The cemetery is the wealthiest place in the world." Many people have died before doing what they were supposed to, whether that be writing a book or finding the cure for cancer. They died without experiencing the riches that come from fulfilling one's purpose.*

In his book, Single, Married, Separated and Life after Divorce, *Dr. Myles Munroe describes singleness as wholeness, stating that we are not fully ready to be married until we are fully whole as single people. My interpretation of wholeness is healing our brokenness through wise counsel, loving ourselves, and allowing God to define us with His Love for us.*

From a young age, I wanted to be somebody who counsels, heals people's broken hearts, and sets people free from pain. And so that God-given destiny and purpose was always bigger than me. I was motivated to study psychology and had faith that God would open up this avenue despite achieving average grades in high school and my undergraduate degree. I qualified as a clinical psychologist despite many obstacles. As a female, I also felt it was my purpose to help women who feel empty without a partner and to assist those who go from one dysfunctional partner to another.

If I had gotten married in my twenties, I would not have qualified as a psychologist because I would have been preoccupied with finding a job, purchasing a home, and planning for parenthood. I think I would have been miserable, feeling stuck and unfulfilled since I would not have maximized my potential and would have had an unrealistic expectation of what a husband should be.

Some people expect their spouses to fulfill them on a level that only a God-given purpose can. Ironically most of the family members that put pressure on me to get married ended up being unhappy in their marriages and unfortunately got divorced, despite being Christians, too. I noticed that there were many Christian single women caught up in the urgency to get married for fear of stigma and judgment from others, yet there were very few Christian singles as role-models to others.

I met my husband when I was thirty-seven years old. We married when I was thirty-eight years old, and I became pregnant soon after. God's timing was once again perfect. Being married now, I give my single friends this advice: "Do lots of things that you're not going to get a chance to do once you get married—get busy with what you were born to do." My husband is amazing. I believe we share a common purpose to help others through counselling and share other common values, too. However, he is not the source of my fulfillment; God is still my Source.

My advice: Get busy with trying to make a difference in the world. Find a purpose bigger than yourself, and don't be afraid to go where God leads you.

—ANNIE, FORTY-FIVE YEARS OLD, SOUTH AFRICA

USING YOUR SINGLE SEASON AS A TIME FOR SERVICE

So far, in this book, we have traveled quite a journey together. We discussed tools to use to overcome frustration about our singleness. We looked at where our confusion about our marital status is coming from and how we can get clarity on the issues. We've reviewed the keys to handling loneliness, to overcoming self-doubt, and to becoming a whole person. And together, we've explored our past experiences, our hurts, our needs, and who we are as singles. We are now ready to move forward and to look at what we should do in our season of singleness.

I have no idea how long I will stay single. It may be just one more year before I have an amazing encounter with the woman who will become the love of my life. You may remain single for only another month or two until a charming, attractive man or woman comes up to your table where you are sipping coffee and pursues you in the most honoring way possible. Or it may take much longer for us to find our mates. We don't know. But, in the meantime, we should consider the purpose of our single season. Should we be doing more as a single person than trying to find our soulmates?

The short answer is, "Yes."

The Bible presents many men and women who were single for a season and some who remained unmarried for their entire lives. For example, Moses was single for a long season before meeting his soulmate, Zipporah, when fleeing Pharaoh into the wastelands. Daniel was apparently single his entire life, or at least we find no mention of any relationships he may have had. David, Joseph, and Isaac were singles for a season, too. Anna was a widow for a long time. And don't forget the apostle Paul, who was single for his entire life. All of these men and women accomplished much while they were single.

In a sermon I once heard, a pastor asked, "Who is more available to go to somewhere like Haiti to bring relief after an earthquake: a single person or a married person? If you are single, you can head out to help within a few days, because you only need to tell your boss where you're going. You simply take an extended vacation, and you leave. Married people can't do that."

His sermon made me reflect. Before that, I had not taken the time to consider all of the benefits of being single. Instead, I'd looked upon my singleness as a burden, something I had to endure. For example, I had long wished to move to a different country but didn't do so out of fear I might miss meeting my future wife if I left. My singleness made me stay put. That's also the reason I would have never agreed to go to Haiti or another remote country to offer my help after a natural disaster. What would happen if my soulmate showed up at my church, but I missed her because I was serving on a mission abroad? I let being single hold me back from doing things I wanted to do.

Furthermore, I didn't understand I was supposed to have a specific purpose as a single, a mission from God, so I missed the opportunity to create momentum as a consistent change-maker. I imagine what I could have accomplished if I'd begun doing His work twenty years ago and regret not pushing myself to take more risks earlier in my single season.

How different would our world be if we single people stopped spending so much energy trying to find our soulmate? What would happen if we followed the prophet Isaiah's example?

> *And I heard the voice of the Lord saying, "Whom shall I send, and who will go for us?" Then I said, "Here I am! Send me."*
>
> **—ISAIAH 6:8**

God's call has not stopped since the time of Isaiah. He is still looking for people serving Him and willing to go all in. And I am convinced that God has a unique plan for us singles. Why? Because we are available. Nowadays, single people stay single longer, and God wants to leverage our extra time so that we each leave a legacy: a lasting good deed that we do for others. Have you imagined what impact you could have in the time you are single? You are right if you feel married people can—and should—leave a legacy, too. That is 100 percent true. God wants to use all of us to our fullest extent. But I believe in our single season, God can uniquely use us. As singles, we can make a massive difference. "Doing what?" you may ask. Let's turn to the Bible to look for answers about our purpose.

FOLLOWING ADAM'S EXAMPLE OF SERVICE TO GOD

When I read the Book of Genesis, I imagine Adam thinking, "There must be someone else on this earth similar to me. Will I meet that person today?"

And then God called him and said, "I have an important task for you to do. I know you like observing animals, so I want you to name each of them for me."

I bet Adam was excited about this job. He saw the thousands of animals lined up, walking toward him, and understood that every animal came in two different versions: male and female. So, logically he assumed that he, too, had a partner somewhere in the group. Unfortunately, throughout the entire naming process, he did not find anyone like himself. In fact, Adam did not meet Eve until later, when God put him to sleep and fashioned her from one of his ribs.

Why didn't God give Adam a companion right away? At the end of creation, God said everything was very good, but how could that be if Adam was still mate-less? Giving names to all the animals was a monumental task with great responsibility, and yet God had Adam do it alone, without Eve. Why?

I think God may have wanted to show us that he has an order for things. He deliberately had Adam name the animals alone first, before he met Eve, to show that singles have responsibilities and missions from God, too. God wants you to fill your single season with a purpose. He dreams that you go all in and use your talents, energy, time, and resources while you are single, following the example of Adam.

FINDING GOD'S MISSION FOR YOU

God placed us here to contribute to His great works of salvation and restoration. He could have done it all by Himself. After all, He is God. But instead, He gave us the mission to spread His gospel and to make disciples for Him. He wants us to participate and rejoice in His salvation of all mankind, which is a monumental mission. Making a big difference like that is no easy task. It requires much thought, effort, courage, persistence, bet-the-farm risk-taking, tolerance, and time. But imagine living your single season in such a way people could come to know Jesus through you. How great would that be?

As a single person, you could live for yourself and become busy being busy. Marketer, author, and columnist, Ryan Holiday said, "This is a fundamental irony of most people's lives. They don't quite know what they want to do with their lives. Yet they are very active." Are you busy being busy? Take a look at your screen time. How much time do you waste on social media searching for your better half? If you repurposed that time to help others and do God's work, you could make a big difference. And now is the perfect time for you to do good works before you become involved with a spouse and children. Like Paul, you could take advantage of your singleness:

An unmarried man can spend his time doing the Lord's work and thinking how to please him. But a married man has to think about his earthly responsibilities and how to please his wife.

—1 CORINTHIANS 7:32-33 (NLT)

Could it be that God is giving you more time during your single season to allow you to serve Him by helping others? Your life does not have to be just about finding a soulmate, settling down, and having kids. Don't get me wrong—there's nothing wrong with those ideals. But rather than focusing on them, I challenge you to expand your goals and desires. Look at what you can do to serve God and your fellow man now, while you are free of the responsibilities of having a family.

DISCOVERING GOD'S MISSION FOR ME

In November 2014, my brother and I flew to Singapore and Cambodia to enjoy a couple of days in their hot and sunny weather before returning to the cold and dark winter days back home. As we walked through the streets of Phnom Penh, the capital of Cambodia, the pervasive poverty caused me to have an "I can't stand this!" moment. Pastor and author Bill Hybels often speaks of "holy discontent," and that phrase summed up my feelings that day: a blend of anger, disappointment, and despair. I reflected on how the children and youth of that country could be shown a brighter future filled with opportunities, hope, prosperity, and peace. Walking past a university campus, a thought crossed my mind: "What if we offered English classes to young Cambodians?" Because so many great internet resources are available in English, teaching the children that language would open many doors of opportunity for them. By contrast, next to nothing is available on the internet in the Cambodian language of Khmer. I kept mulling over this idea for the rest of my vacation and continued for a little while when I returned home. But then I became busy with my daily life and forgot all about it.

And then, in 2016, I led a mission team to a church and non-governmental organization in Siem Reap, Cambodia. During my stay, the idea of teaching English resurfaced. "We should invest in education,"

I said to the local pastor. I explained that I felt educating children was proactive and would provide them with the tools they needed for a better future.

He liked the idea but said they lacked funding for such an effort. "David, if you find the money, we'll be happy to start a training program here."

"It's a deal!" I said. My heart rate skyrocketed with excitement about having a purpose greater than myself. I knew it was the right thing to do. Within a few weeks, I was able to raise enough money to start a trial with three students who got the opportunity to attend a private school and have apprenticeships within the organization. Through the program, they learned English and were able to use that knowledge to successfully unlock the vast educational resources available in that language on the internet. The program was a success. Today, twenty-eight students are enrolled in the training program and can benefit from a good education.

REALIZING YOU SHOULDN'T PLAY IT SAFE

Nothing will fill your heart with a greater sense of regret than lying on your deathbed knowing that you did not live your life so as to realize your dreams.

—ROBIN SHARMA, AUTHOR AND MOTIVATIONAL SPEAKER

There is a spiritual battle going on. The devil knows what breath-taking potential you possess, and so he tries to discourage you from using it. Alternatively, he will put enticing activities in your path to distract you, such as the new Netflix series that everybody is binge-watching. When I was younger, I watched every TV episode of *Friends* and *The Simpsons*. I enjoyed them, but I wasted too much time on them. If I had capitalized on a fraction of the time I spent in front of the screen back then, I might have a highly successful blog or other business running by now.

The devil also tries to keep you in your comfort zone, knowing taking risks may scare you. He hopes your fear will paralyze you and keep you from meeting your awesome potential. By contrast, God encourages us to branch out and do the unexpected. He wants us to use our talents to serve Him by helping others.

Making a lot of money and moving up the career ladder never interested me. I often said, "I don't live to work; I work to live." In my thirties, though, I sensed God nudging me to change the path of my career. Since I thought He frowned on people focusing too much on themselves and their professional lives, I couldn't figure out what He wanted me to do. For nearly three years, I kept feeling God prodding me to change my heart but couldn't figure out in what direction He wanted me to go. Then I attended a service at a megachurch in Singapore during a business trip and received a revelation. The pastor talked about influence and asked the businesspeople to stand up and said, "This is your ministry: God called you to build His Kingdom in the marketplace." In other words, He wanted us to use our business skills to do more than just make a living. He wanted us to use them to work for Him. Because of my career, I had a unique skillset available to me. And because I was in my single season, I had time available to use my skills to great effect. I had never seen my life and career from this perspective before.

Churches often leave businesspeople on the sidelines and don't include them in ministries because pastors don't know what to do with them. Likewise, churches have not tapped into the potential of long-term single people. However, God recognizes the value of both segments of the congregation and wants to use us in unique ways to serve Him, ways that we may not think of on our own. God has great things in store for you. He will amaze you. So, buckle up and prepare yourself for the ride of your life. On the other side of comfortable, you will experience miraculous.

I dream of a new generation of fulfilled singles who go all in and change this world for good. What if God gave you this gift of extended singleness so you may have a bigger impact on the world around you? Could it be he wants you and me to take on more responsibility and make bigger changes? Does He want to use you in a full-fledged mission in much bigger ways than you ever have imagined? Are you ready for a shakeup? You don't get to play it safe any longer. God wants you to pray dangerous prayers, like this one:

Disturb me, Lord, when I'm too well pleased with myself, when my dreams have come true. Because I have dreamed too little, when I arrived safely. Because I sailed too close to the shore.

—SIR FRANCIS DRAKE, SEA CAPTAIN, NAVAL OFFICER, AND EXPLORER

God has a unique role for you and me. He wants us to leverage our skills and our availability to advance His Kingdom. He wants to give your life meaning as He did with Adam. He loves to provide you with a great task in this season of your life. But you cannot play it safe. You must see being single as a God-given gift, one that you can offer back to Him in service. When we give what we have, miracles happen. Do you remember the gospel story of the small boy who brought his five loaves of bread and two fish to Jesus? The Son of God took the modest gift, multiplied it, and fed 5,000 people. In the same way, God wants to multiply your influence. Are you ready to take up the challenge? Are you ready for more?

PROVIDING NEW VISIONS FOR SINGLES

You and I need to help provide new visions for singles. In *The Message* Bible translation, we read:

If people can't see what God is doing, they stumble all over themselves.

—PROVERBS 29:18 (MSG)

Ladies and gentlemen, it's time for us to actively formulate a new mission for singles: one in which we thrive. It seems that many churches don't have a vision for their unmarried congregants. If you develop a new vision for yourself and the other singles in your church, you can discuss it with your single friends and then with your pastor. In this way, you will play a pivotal role in helping your church gain a new perspective on the place of singles in the community. How great is that?

But let us aim even higher. Let's promote an exchange of ideas that provides the framework for meaningful change in our churches and, by extension, in the world around us. Let's build a community of single people who want to make a difference. I invite you to email me at david@singleforaseason.com with your new vision ideas. I would love to mention them on my blog. Through this interaction, we could begin to create a community that supports each other in these new efforts. I'm looking forward to receiving your ideas to make this dream a reality.

GETTING A NEW VISION FROM GOD

For many years, I tried to live my life per the visions of my friends, family, and society. In my thirties, I wanted to get married as soon as possible because that's what others told me I should do. I did not take the time to ask God what He wanted. Nowadays, I do, and I know He has things under control.

God gave me the vision to make a difference in Cambodia, a country that had never even been on my radar before. By listening to Him and following His prompts, I have found deep fulfillment in pursuing my mission here. He provided me with a new vision, and now I leverage my time to serve the Cambodian people during my single season.

God has a purpose for you, too, and wants you to give you a new vision. But you must ask Him for it and look for it first. Consider the story of the prophet Habakkuk. He said:

I will take my stand at my watchpost and station myself on the tower, and look out to see what he will say to me, and what I will answer concerning my complaint.

—HABAKKUK 2:1

Habakkuk's story highlights an important point: He did not just complain. Instead, he took action and put himself in a place where he could hear God speaking to him. Why? Because he was searching for guidance from God and was expecting it. His conviction enabled him to hear His words.

And the Lord answered me.

—HABAKKUK 2:2

If we keep looking for God's assistance, we will receive it, so don't give up. Keep inviting Him to speak to you until you hear Him. He promised this to Habakkuk:

> *Write the vision; make it plain on tablets, so he may run who reads it. For still the vision awaits its appointed time; it hastens to the end—it will not lie. If it seems slow, wait for it; it will surely come; it will not delay.*
>
> **—HABAKKUK 2:2-3**

God gave him a new direction. And He will do the same for you, too. Of course, you may have to be patient because God will provide what you need, when you need it, in His time, not yours. But when He does, as a bonus, by sharing your experience with single friends of yours, you can help them find the new vision for their single season, too. How cool is that? You get a new vision for your life and influence others to receive theirs, so they can thrive, too. Or, as Paul said, "I press on toward the goal for the prize of the upward call of God in Christ Jesus" (Philippians 3:14).

SACRIFICING FOR GOD'S VISION

I'm a little pencil in the hand of a writing God, who is sending a love letter to the world.

—MOTHER TERESA, NUN AND MISSIONARY

To become a purposeful single person, you must heed God's vision for you, even if this comes at the expense of your personal needs and security. The people who change the world often must make tremendous sacrifices. During the COVID-19 pandemic, many such heroes emerged. One Italian nurse posted a selfie showing bruises on her face due to the personal protective equipment she had to wear during her thirteen-hour shifts. She worked tirelessly in the intensive care unit, taking care of patients in critical condition. She did not allow the exhausting, stressful conditions or the risk of infection to keep her from helping them. In China, a well-known physician finally succumbed to the disease after working long shifts with inadequate protective gear. He worked for as long as he could to save as many patients as possible without regard for his personal safety because he felt that was his calling.

Living with purpose by following the vision given to us by God sometimes requires enormous sacrifices. Are you ready for that? Jesus promises if we lose our life, we will gain it. Service to others gives you a deep sense of fulfillment in knowing that you are doing what God intended for you to do.

REASSESSING YOUR PRIORITIES

Should my priority in life be to find my soulmate, or should I set aside that desire to focus on making a more considerable difference in the world, such as the work I'm doing in Cambodia? This was a difficult question for me to answer. I would have liked to say, "Yes, of course, I want to make a big difference," but when I listened to the voice deep down in my heart, I knew part of me still wanted to find that special someone and get married.

At least for now, I am willing to forgo my active search for a soulmate in favor of pursuing my vision to improve the level of education available in Cambodia. In fact, I view my singleness as a benefit for me right now, allowing me to concentrate on the important work I am doing in Cambodia. (More about that in Chapter 12.) My priority is making a difference in the world. That is what gets me up in the morning and makes me believe I am doing what God intended me to do in this single season.

Making a difference is an intentional choice that I must make every day. I challenge you to consider whether you could make a difference, too. Do you feel a burden because of human trafficking, hunger, burnout, depression, the millions of people who have not heard the gospel, one-parent families, climate change, lack of education, homelessness, drug abuse, or suicide? Or maybe God has laid your local community on your heart. You see how people are sleeping on the streets even on the coldest days of the year when the thermometer falls well below freezing and wonder how they can survive. You know that someone should do something about it. And then you realize that someone is you. That's where you can make a difference.

CHAPTER 7: WRAP-UP

When trying to determine your purpose as a single, remember there are no limits to what you can accomplish. Don't let anyone tell you that you cannot do what you have on your heart: not your friends, family, or even your pastor. No one. If God gave you a vision of what you should do, then go for it. Leverage your knowledge, your wisdom, your finances, your passion, and your time as a single person to make a difference and make this world a better place.

CHAPTER 7: TAKEAWAYS

FINDING YOUR PURPOSE AS A SINGLE PERSON

POINTS TO CONSIDER

1. God wants you to fill your single season with purpose and meaning. He has a unique plan for you that exceeds the search for your soulmate. In this season, you can work to create an eternal legacy: a footprint of the good you did while a resident of this planet.

2. It's tempting to stay in your comfort zone because that's the easy thing to do. But God dreams of you going all in and using your talents, energy, time, and resources to advance His Kingdom.

3. Making a difference is an intentional choice. Although such a lifestyle requires sacrifices, it gives you joy and a deep sense of fulfillment.

QUESTIONS FOR GROUPS

1. If you had all the money and time to do whatever you wanted, what would you do?

2. What cause do you feel God has laid on your heart? What does He want you to do?

3. How do you find a balance between your search for your soulmate and your quest to find your higher purpose?

ACTION STEPS TO TAKE

1. Read this dangerous prayer:

Disturb me, Lord, when I'm too well pleased with myself, when my dreams have come true. Because I have dreamed too little, when I arrived safely. Because I sailed too close to the shore.

**—SIR FRANCIS DRAKE, SEA CAPTAIN,
NAVAL OFFICER, AND EXPLORER**

2. Reflect upon its meaning and how you could apply it to your life.

CHAPTER 8

REALIZING YOU ARE NOT MISSING OUT

Never be afraid to trust an unknown future to a known God.

—CORRIE TEN BOOM, WRITER AND EVANGELIST

STORY OF A SINGLE

The older I get, the more I fear, "Will I end up never realizing my dreams of having a husband and children?" Keeping my hopes up for a year or two is doable. But after fifteen years of singleness, it's challenging to keep believing. I sometimes struggle to understand God's timing, too, asking, "When is God going to help me?"

I've prayed much, hoped much. I know that faith is the belief in things you can't see, but when it comes to my desire to have children and the famous biological clock that's ticking, I struggle to maintain that faith.

When I was young, God laid my dream to become a mother on my heart. I received a vision, seeing myself on a hill with a man next to me with a child on his shoulders and three children surrounding us. That's why maintaining my faith is difficult. How can I have children at my age? Over the years, I have put aside this dream because I lose hope. But then it comes back even though, biologically speaking, I know it's impossible.

When I was thirty-eight years old, I fell in love with a guy of a different religion. Although he wasn't the sort of man I wanted as a husband and a father to my future children, I chose to start a relationship with him anyway. For four years now, I have been struggling with our relationship, and at the same time, to my surprise, I have developed a special closeness with God. I know I have to stop the unhealthy relationship with this guy. But paralyzing fear has prevented me from doing the right thing. I'm afraid without him, I will have no one. I will never get married and will never have children.

At the same time, I feel like I don't have to worry because God has everything under control. I have discovered His grace and goodness. As long as my heart is with God, and I make Him my priority in life, I know He will walk with me. What's the most important thing in my life? What directs my life? Where do I find my happiness? What is my joy? Where do I get my strength and my hope? I realize all of these are from God, not my potential spouse.

At forty-two years of age, I have to take a leap of faith, not knowing if it means I'm going to be single for the rest of my life. I thought a lot about my decision and talked it over with my life coach. She said, "It's clear to me that you will get married, and it's clear to me that you've learned how to be single, too."

Through prayer, God did tremendous work giving me strength and showing me what was important. He put people in my life who helped me to move forward. I still do not understand His plan for my life, but He has revealed Himself to me in a new way. As a result, God set me free, and I'm regaining trust in Him.

—VÉRONIQUE, FORTY-TWO YEARS OLD, SWITZERLAND

DEALING WITH SHATTERED DREAMS

What do you do if your dream of finding a soulmate does not come true? You did everything right: prayed, went to counseling, read relationship books, put your best picture on an online dating platform, and even discovered your purpose as a single, but yet you have not found a lasting relationship. You look around and see people who are getting married and having children. Do you believe you are missing out?

According to Luke's Gospel, everything in Anna's life was going according to plan. She and her boyfriend got engaged and then were married in a beautiful ceremony, attended by friends and family. Their first few years as a young couple were even more amazing than she had imagined. They started preparing for the children they planned to have together. Smiling at her handsome husband with his curly dark brown hair, she asked him, "Who do you think they will look like more? You or me?"

Then one day in their seventh year of marriage, Anna's husband complained of not feeling well. He was pale and running a fever, so she tucked him into bed, saying, "Get some rest. I'm sure you'll feel better in the morning." Instead, his condition deteriorated rapidly. His fever skyrocketed and every breath became difficult. Worried, Anna sent for a doctor, but her young husband died before help arrived.

With her husband's death, Anna's dreams were shattered, and she also lost all her hopes for a secure future, because, in her country of Israel, a widow's life was very difficult. Luke wrote that after her husband's death, Anna remained a widow for the rest of her long life—eighty-four years, which was considered quite old 2,000 years ago. She never got remarried and never had children, so she probably felt like she was missing out on many of the dreams she had as a young woman.

FEELING LIKE WE ARE MISSING OUT

Why do we sometimes feel like we are missing out on something in life? I believe the answer to that question comes down to identifying what we believe is the most critical thing to us. If we lack what we perceive as the most important element in our lives but see others around us who have it, we feel bereft and cheated.

All through my twenties and thirties, I saw my friends having fun with their soulmates, and moving on to fulfilling lives with beautiful families while I was stuck in my singleness. I felt I was missing out. "I'm a loser," I thought. "I don't get to enjoy the richness of a life of two-ness." Over time, I became desperate and fearful that I wouldn't be able to fully catch up with my friends or—even worse—may never obtain what I wanted most: a soulmate and a family. I was miserable because I was comparing my life with theirs and concentrating on all that I was lacking.

When I was a kid, I remember being afraid that I might miss out on things, too. Specifically, I recall being fearful of not getting any of my mom's Swiss-style fruit pie, one of my favorite dishes. While my dad would pray over our meal, I would stare at the delicious pieces of the pie, sitting on plates, ready to be eaten. Apparently, my two brothers did the same thing because one millisecond after Dad said the magic word "amen," we each reached out at supersonic speed and grabbed one of the pieces. All of us were fearful of missing out on getting some pie. Our parents were there at the table with us, but yet we didn't trust them to ensure that we each got a piece.

It's like that with our Father in Heaven, too. Sometimes we don't trust Him to give us what we want. That's the problem and the reason that we often feel like we are missing out: God gives us what we *need*, which is not necessarily the same as what we *want*. We need to trust Him to understand the difference.

Another component of feeling like we are missing out on something occurs when we compare what we have with what others possess. Looking around, we might think, "It's not fair! Jeff has a brilliant wife and two adorable kids." Being single, we may feel as if Jeff has a much better life than we do. It would be advantageous for us to look at this situation in another way by replacing the word "better" with "different," as in, "Jeff has a *different* life than I do." God gives each of us what we need when we need it, which may not be the same as the gifts our friends and neighbors receive from Him. Don't waste your time comparing your life to the lives of others. Your life is different. Trust God to provide for you as He does for all His children.

REALIZING THE DANGERS OF THE FEAR OF MISSING OUT

If you suffer from the fear of missing out (FOMO), you dwell in a dangerous place. FOMO makes us miserable and may lead us to make stupid decisions.

In the Book of Genesis, we hear about Adam and Eve, who lived in Eden, the most beautiful place that ever existed on planet Earth.

There, they enjoyed eating delicious fruits, with nearly any variety they could imagine available whenever they wanted it.

God told them, "You may freely eat the fruit of every tree in the garden, except the Tree of the Knowledge of Good and Evil."

It was one tree among many hundreds—maybe even thousands— of trees, and yet the snake managed to turn their eyes towards it by goading them to experience FOMO.

"Why can't we eat that amazing fruit, Eve?" Adam may have asked when taking her for a walk one cold evening.

She might have said, "They look so yummy. I want to try them now." And in that instant, the world saw the first human beings suffering the consequences of FOMO. Since that time, this fear has become an integral part of our human nature. Hence, I'm not surprised that we singles suffer from it, too. "If I don't get married soon, I will miss the best part of my life!" you may say—a clear case of FOMO.

Because Adam and Eve concentrated on what they were missing, they didn't recognize the lie the snake told them, which led them to be forced to leave the garden. FOMO precipitated that tragedy and can cause pain and unhappiness in your life, too.

UNDERSTANDING WHY YOU ARE NOT MISSING OUT

You'll wait. You'll pray. You'll get frustrated. You'll question everything. But you'll continue to be patient. You'll keep waiting. And you'll keep praying. And one day, when you least expect it, it'll finally happen. So, don't ever stop believing.

Don't ever stop trusting. And don't ever stop hoping. God is so ready to give you everything you've ever dreamed of.

—MANDY HALE, AUTHOR AND SPEAKER

Even though it might seem like you are missing out on some of the good things of life during your singleness, in fact, this season provides you with ample gifts and rewards that more than make up for your perceived deficits. Consider the following reasons for rejoicing:

Reason #1: No One Directs Your Life Better Than God

Do you remember Anna's story from Luke's Gospel discussed at the beginning of this chapter? Did she miss out on the good things of life? Let's see how her story continues.

After the tragic twist of her life, she made the temple her home, serving as a prophetess there. One morning she saw a couple approaching with their baby. As they got closer, she realized that the baby was the Messiah all Jews had been waiting for. Anna was jubilant. According to the gospel:

Coming up at that very hour she began to give thanks to God and to speak of him to all who were waiting for the redemption of Jerusalem.

—LUKE 2:38

175

Anna may not have realized her girlhood dream of having a family, but God more than made it up to her by allowing her to meet the infant Jesus and be there for His presentation at the temple. God had a special plan for Anna and revealed it to her.

Like Anna, we all must trust God to show us His plan for our lives. Realize He is all-knowing, and His plan is perfect.

> *And we know that for those who love God all things work together for good, for those who are called according to his purpose.*
>
> **—ROMANS 8:28**

Even if you feel overlooked, remember God's promise. Your Father in Heaven weaves together every detail of your life, including your dream to live in a romantic relationship. Following His plan will allow you to live the best life possible.

Reason #2: By Letting Go, You Embrace God's Perfect Plan

I'm not suggesting that you forget your dream. I believe we should recognize our desire to be married, but we should never let it become our sole focus: our idol. We must remember our ultimate goal in life is to serve God. We can do that when we are single, divorced, widowed, or married.

In the Book of Genesis, Abraham complained about missing

out on an important part of life because he never had a son. When God finally granted him his son, Isaac, at age one hundred, the answer to Abraham's prayers became his idol upon whom he lavished all his attention. One day, God issued a command to Abraham: "Take your son, your only son, Isaac, whom you love, and go to the land of Moriah, and offer him" (Genesis 22:2). In this way, God told Abraham that he must obey His will and serve Him no matter what he may want to do instead. When Abraham did as commanded, God was pleased.

"By myself I have sworn, declares the Lord, because you have done this and have not withheld your son, your only son, I will surely bless you, and I will surely multiply your offspring."

—GENESIS 22:16-17

If we focus exclusively on our dream of getting married, we will miss out on what God plans for us to do during our single season. But by trusting in His perfect plan for our life, we will reap the rewards He has in store.

Reason #3: When You Put God First, Miracles Happen

When we put God first, miracles happen. In the words of the Psalmist:

> *Give God the right to direct your life, and as you trust him along the way you'll find he pulled it off perfectly!*
>
> **—PSALM 37:5 (TPT)**

We cannot instantly change our relationship status from "single" to "married." Heaven knows we often may want to. And some of us have endured an extended single season, which can be very frustrating. But in the grand scheme of things, this doesn't matter because finding someone special is not the key to overcoming the fear of missing out. The only way to do that is to turn your back from the lack and toward the One who gives abundance. The Psalmist wrote, "Make God the utmost delight" (Psalm 37:4 [TPT]). That is how we overcome FOMO: by understanding God wants the best for our lives, and He always has our best interests in mind, which is not to say He delivers on our every request. Sometimes He does not give us what we want because the time is not right. Sometimes He wants us to grow more first. At other times, our wishes are not fulfilled because God plans to give us something even better than we imagined. However, in the end, He will provide for all our needs, and we will not miss out on all the good that He has in store for us.

You may ask me, "How in the world can you promise me I will never miss out?" I am not a prophet, nor am I one of those speakers who guarantees wealth if you do a few simple steps. But I am quoting a promise Jesus made at His longest recorded speech, the Sermon on the Mount. He said:

Steep your life in God-reality, God-initiative, God-provisions. Don't worry about missing out. You'll find all your everyday human concerns will be met.

—MATTHEW 6:33 (MSG)

If we put God first, we will not miss out. It does not mean that you'll get the Ferrari, the beautiful house, the dream job, the magic encounter with your future soulmate, or other things you've requested in your prayers. What Jesus is saying is this: "Stop this comparison game that makes you desperate. Instead, focus on the relationship with your perfect Father in Heaven, who knows us better than we know ourselves."

Make God the utmost delight and pleasure of your life, and he will provide for you what you desire the most.

—PSALM 37:4 (TPT)

Reason #4: God's Gifts Will Overflow Your Cup

In Psalm 23:5, David wrote that his cup overflowed, which was his way of saying that he was not missing out on anything. Likewise, James, the half-brother of Jesus, made a compelling point in his epistle, saying:

Every good gift and every perfect gift is from above, coming down from the Father of lights, with whom there is no variation or shadow due to change.

—JAMES 1:17

I want to receive God's perfect gifts in all seasons of my life, especially while single. So, why do I sometimes forget God has a perfect plan for my life, whether I'm single or not? Perhaps I lose sight of His omnipotent goodness and become afraid He has forgotten me and my needs. Our enemy is trying to make us believe we lack something as singles, but this tactic—FOMO—is nothing new: even Adam and Eve bought into this fallacy, causing them to eat the forbidden fruit.

Paul's overall attitude impresses me. He could have presented a lot of evidence to show he was missing out: He spent many days of his life in various prisons as punishment for his beliefs and often experienced life-threatening situations during his frequent missionary trips. And yet there is no record of Paul ever complaining. By all accounts, he lived a fulfilled life, and his awareness of God's goodness filled his heart with joy. Consider this: While enduring yet another prison sentence, Paul wrote to the believers in Philippi, "Rejoice in the Lord always; again, I will say, rejoice" (Philippians 4:4). That sure doesn't sound like a man suffering from FOMO.

Reason #5: God Draws You Close to Him

God is more interested in my relationship with Him than in whether or not I am going to marry one day. And when I intentionally strive to get closer to God through prayer and doing His work, He provides me with supernatural encounters with Him, the God of the Universe. That's when He changes my heart, makes me forget FOMO, and helps me realize I am living my life to the fullest. If I look at what I want and feel I am missing, I feel the lack, but when I keep my eyes fixed on God, I see His spiritual reality.

> *Draw near to God, and he will draw near to you.*
>
> **—JAMES 4:8**

My singleness forces me to draw near to Him to seek His guidance. As a result, God draws near to me, so I never miss out on a single thing. His goodness exceeds anything I can imagine. When I trust Him, He embraces me, opens the gates of heaven, and pours out His blessings over me.

Reason #6: Your Desires Will Align with God's

In the Common English Bible, Psalm 37:4 says, "Enjoy the LORD, and he will give you what your heart asks." This means as we bask in God's attention, something unexpected takes place: our desires change. As we spend more time with Him, we understand what He wants for us. That is the best remedy to decrease our frustrations over what we lack, because the more we align our desires with His, the more we get what we want. If our desires diverge, He may say, "No," to protect us, but He will grant our requests if they agree with His plan, knowing that this is best for us.

Reason #7: Even If I Did Miss Out, God Can Turn the Situation Around

God can take what Satan meant for shame and use it for His glory. Just when we think we've messed up so badly that our lives are nothing but heaps of ashes, God pours His living water over us and mixes the ashes into clay. He then takes this clay and molds it into a vessel of beauty. After He fills us with His overflowing love, He can use us to pour His love into the hurting lives of others.

—LYSA TERKEURST, PRESIDENT OF PROVERBS 31 MINISTRIES

My roommate invited me to a singles night at his church. Even though I often found such events awkward, I said, "Yes." When we arrived, I spotted a beautiful woman with long brown hair arranged very attractively. Soon, I was speaking with her and another woman, although I found I was conversing much more with her talkative friend. The brown-haired woman was quiet but looked intriguing, and I made sure to get her phone number.

I contacted her after the event, and, about two weeks later, we had our first date, which left me with a mixed impression. At that time, I was desperate for a girlfriend, so fearing I would miss the opportunity for a relationship, I asked her out again a few times despite our less-than-stellar first date. Long story short, I eventually realized I made the wrong decision and missed out on what could have been a better relationship with the woman's talkative friend. Like Jacob—who, in desperation, offered to work seven years to earn the right to marry Rachel, the woman he loved—I forgot I should listen to God since He had my best interests at heart. Like the Israelites who coveted the idols of their neighbors, I put my desire for a girlfriend first, even though it pushed God away, prevented me from living my life to the fullest, and caused me to suffer a bout of FOMO. Big mistake.

Because of invaluable lessons learned through His counsel, I came out of this failure better than I entered it. And, I can now use those lessons to help other singles thrive. Even though the brown-haired woman and I stopped seeing each other and I am single again, I don't feel like I'm missing out. Instead, God turned the situation around and allowed my experience to pave the way for greater things, including my blog and this book, *Single for a Season*, which will hopefully help others live a more fulfilled life.

Reason #8: God's Gift Is Always Better

Acknowledge that you are single and therefore different from your married friends. Understand your singleness is a gift from God, and since it is a gift, you are not missing out, but are getting more than you expected.

God is good all the time. He is our caring Father. Think about your own experience. Do you see God doing great things in your life? Remind yourself of all the wonderful things He does for you. This will help you to stand firm when the going gets tough—when your FOMO-lie kicks in.

Reason #9: You May Embrace the Advantages of Single Life

One day a guy was talking with his pastor, "You are so lucky! You have been married for years and now you have children. What more could you want?"

The pastor seemed annoyed. "I think *you* are the lucky one."

"I?"

"Yes. You enjoy so much more freedom than I do. You can decide to have a spontaneous drink with your friends after work while I have to go home to take care of my children."

What one man considered the burden of singleness, the other perceived as the freedom of not being married.

In a recent online single hangout, one of the participants asked a great question: "How would your life change if you could forget all about your desire to get married?" I think if we stopped dwelling on our singleness, we would no longer feel as if we were missing out. And like my friend, Sopheap, who shared her story in Chapter 6, I believe it would enable us to enjoy the multiple advantages of this wonderful single season of life.

I like the way I spend my time, now. I can choose who I want to spend time with and when I want to be by myself. When I compare my life to the lives of couples and families, I recognize theirs are more complicated. For now, at least, I prefer the freedom of my single season.

Reason #10: You Learn Patience

We live in a world of instant gratification. With the advent of cellphones and the internet, our society is used to getting things immediately. Unfortunately, I have not found the "Perfect Girlfriend Now" button on my phone or TV remote. (If you have, please contact me right away.) And when I don't feel the companionship and loving affection enjoyed by my married friends, I fear I'm missing out.

One of the big lessons I had to learn as a single is the necessity of being patient. Love often doesn't come to us right away. But that doesn't mean we are missing out. Think about the last time you were waiting in line to order your food at your favorite take-out restaurant. Did you think you were missing out if you had to wait for five minutes before placing your order? Probably not. Because you knew you would soon have your food, you didn't mind waiting. You knew what you were waiting for was going to arrive. However, I am not 100 percent certain that I'm ever going to meet my soulmate. If I knew two years from now I would meet her at a friend's birthday party, my feeling of missing out would disappear. But since I'm uncertain and since I'm not making any progress in the girlfriend department, I feel I may be missing something important, and worse, something I will not be able to get later. I need to trust that God will provide what I want, and I must be patient. And that is the hard part. Learning patience is definitely not my favorite course in the school of life. I wish I could skip it. However, I must admit, through my longer-than-planned single season, I have learned to become more patient.

When you are not getting what you want, it doesn't mean you are missing out. Sometimes, I have the impression God leaves me in this foggy unclarity because He wants me to trust Him more. If I knew what was going to happen, I would not need God. I could prepare myself for my friend's birthday party when I would introduce myself to my future wife with confidence, knowing she would say, "Yes." That would be easy—or, perhaps, too easy. But since I am not clairvoyant, I must rely on God to provide for me, and I must be patient.

Reason #11: You Are Reminded of God's Goodness

When the Israelites crossed the Jordan, God told them to take stones out of the river and to use them for a specific purpose:

When your children ask in time to come, "What do those stones mean to you?" then you shall tell them that the waters of the Jordan were cut off before the Ark of the Covenant of the Lord. When it passed over the Jordan, the waters of the Jordan were cut off. So, these stones shall be to the people of Israel a memorial forever.

—JOSHUA 4:6-7

God knew when things got tough, His people would think they were missing out. He commanded them to build the monument to remind them of what He had done for them.

As singles, we also need to remind ourselves of all the wonderful things God has done for us. We are in a constant battle with our enemy, who tries to rob us of the peace God wants to give us. The media, our friends, and our success-culture all scream: "If you don't live in a relationship, you are not living the way you're supposed to, and you are missing out!" Instead, we need to remember our Father's gifts to us in our single season.

The things we desire today may differ from what the Israelites were seeking, but the underlying reason for FOMO has not changed: we forget that God wants the very best for our lives. So, remember God is looking out for you, and, like the Israelites, you must trust He will provide for you. Mentally build a monument to remind yourself you will never miss out. Never. No matter how bad your circumstances appear at the moment, God will never let you down.

CHAPTER 8: WRAP-UP

Being single in a world where everyone around you seems to be enjoying the great benefits of being in relationships is no easy task and may make you feel like you're missing out on the good things of life. Be aware of cultivating the fear of missing out because letting it grow will only set you up to feel frustrated and make stupid decisions you may regret later.

Despite your feelings of frustration, despite your dire perspectives, despite your failures and regrets that make you believe you've missed the boat, you are *not* missing out. God has a great plan for you. He has not given up on you, nor has He turned His face from you. His promises still stand. When you put God first, you'll never miss out.

However, this does not mean everything will happen according to your desires or your life plan. God is more interested in forging your eternal character than in promoting your temporary well-being. I know that's hard to accept. In the short term, from an earthly perspective, you may miss out on what seems important in this world. From an eternal perspective, however, you will never miss out. Jesus promised us abundant life. Or in the words of David, "My cup overflows" (Psalm 23:5). God still is your miracle maker and capable of turning your situation around.

If you change your focus by fixing your eyes on Jesus instead of what you lack, you'll realize that you're not missing out. God is good all the time. Or in the words of David, "The LORD is good to all, and his mercy is over all that he has made" (Psalm 145:9).

CHAPTER 8: TAKEAWAYS

REALIZING YOU ARE NOT MISSING OUT

POINTS TO CONSIDER

1. If you don't have what you think you need and see others around you who do have it, you feel bereft and cheated, and may get the impression that you are missing out.

2. Fear of missing out (FOMO) is dangerous because it makes you miserable and may lead to you making unwise decisions.

3. Your single season provides you with plenty of gifts and rewards that more than make up for whatever you may feel you lack. Just concentrate on putting God first in your life, and you'll find He takes care of you and makes sure you are definitely not missing out on what's truly important.

QUESTIONS FOR GROUPS

1. What do you feel you are lacking?

2. Why do you fear you are missing out?

3. When do you experience God helping you to get rid of FOMO? Encourage each other by sharing your experiences.

ACTION STEPS TO TAKE

1. Read these passages of Scripture:

2. Psalm 23:1-6: The Lord is my shepherd; I shall not want. He makes me lie down in green pastures. He leads me beside still waters. He restores my soul. He leads me in paths of righteousness for his name's sake. Even though I walk through the valley of the shadow of death, I will fear no evil, for you are with me; your rod and your staff, they comfort me. You prepare a table before me in the presence of my enemies; you anoint my head with oil; my cup overflows. Surely goodness and mercy shall follow me all the days of my life, and I shall dwell in the house of the Lord forever.

3. Matthew 6:33-34: But seek first the kingdom of God and his righteousness, and all these things will be added to you. Therefore do not be anxious about tomorrow, for tomorrow will be anxious for itself. Sufficient for the day is its own trouble.

4. Romans 8:28: And we know that for those who love God all things work together for good, for those who are called according to his purpose.

5. Reflect on their meanings in your life and write about them in your journal.

CHAPTER 9

WAITING IN PEACE

Look carefully then how you walk, not as unwise but as wise, making the best use of the time.

—EPHESIANS 5:15-16

While you're waiting for an answer from God in one area of your life, don't put all the other areas on hold. Watch for where God is giving you direction and go with that. Trust him with the stuff that is still unanswered and keep moving forward. He knows what we don't.

—CHRISTINE CAINE, ACTIVIST, EVANGELIST, AUTHOR, AND SPEAKER

STORY OF A SINGLE

After a five-year relationship ended, I reflected on how I wanted to spend my free time and decided to use it to enhance my education and broaden my horizons. I worked at a full-time job during the day and studied at the University of Applied Sciences in the evenings.

When I completed my studies, I asked myself what I should do next, "Do I continue with regular business, lead more significant projects, accept more responsibility, or try to grow in some other way? Or should I attempt to give back by leaving my comfort zone and spending my time somewhere else learning something new?" After traveling the world, I decided to move to Cambodia to serve the people there, sharing my professional expertise with them.

I don't see my singleness as a waiting period because, during this time, I've learned to be the best I can be—not as a single, but as a person. I believe that God takes care of me, guides me, and shows me what to do next. This helps me relax and prevents unhealthy impatience. I must be open to developing my self-awareness and improving myself continually.

Singleness has its challenges. But I see it as similar to viewing a rug from the bottom, where you see all the knots that hold the rug together. It is only when viewed from the top that the rug's beauty is revealed. In the same way, I believe God is preparing me for what's coming next, tying together all my various pieces to make me the best whole person I can be. And yet, I must take the required steps to continue growing. If I do my part, God will do His. I am grateful for what He gives me. Throughout this whole process, I must stay open to what can happen because through Him miraculous things can occur, things I could never anticipate. For instance, I would not have expected to come to Cambodia two years ago.

—LAURENT, THIRTY-SEVEN YEARS, SWITZERLAND

In this chapter, we will discuss how you can take care of your emotional self and find peace while waiting for your soulmate. Through this process, you will become a better version of yourself, which will make you more attractive and help you avoid feeling desperate.

You and I have a few things in common. For one thing, we are in our single season and have a reason for being in this season. In other words, we have the gift of singleness for a particular time. When anyone asks me if I am married, I answer with a smile, "I'm not married *yet*." My answer reminds me of the temporary nature of my relationship status.

We have another thing in common, too. We all are good-looking, funny, and the most exceptional people on this earth. I'm kidding—a bit!

REMINDERS FOR FINDING PEACE

What follows are some truths about being single I find valuable to remember. Hopefully, they will help you find peace while you are waiting to meet your ideal spouse.

Reminder #1: Even If You Don't Get Married, You'll Be Fine

All my life, I fervently believed I would marry one day. I leveraged everything within my power to make it happen. Over time, I became obsessed with finding my future spouse. Then I got the feeling God was saying, "David, you may have gone a little too far." He pushed me with His gentle hands toward a different path: helping children in Cambodia.

I asked God, "Is this what I'm supposed to do? Do you want me to forget my dream of getting married and focus on Your work, instead?" I hoped these crazy ideas would disappear, but they didn't. Instead, they became so strong I couldn't get them out of my mind.

So, I told Him, "You know what's best for me, so I'll do what You say." Even though it was very difficult for me, trusting God seemed to be the way to go, so I did my best to do His will.

As a young adult and until my early thirties, I was afraid to relinquish my will to Him. "God, I will go wherever you want me to be," felt like a very dangerous prayer to me. What if He sent me to Siberia or someplace like that? I was afraid truly following God would mean giving up everything I liked, doing something I didn't want to do, and living in an ugly and challenging place. And I wasn't convinced I should trust Him regarding my future relationships, either.

Over time, I came to believe God would lead me to places where I could best serve Him. And He has. He's led me into jobs and positions in my church where I've been able to make a difference. But fear still prevented me from letting Him control my relational future. I saw my life happening a certain way, and I didn't trust that He would make things happen to my satisfaction. However, to my surprise, when I finally did relinquish my will to God, He started making miracles happen.

When I say "miracles," I don't mean I've found my soulmate. That miracle has yet to happen. But while I'm waiting for that, God began to pour blessings of a different kind over my life: He's provided peace in my heart, given me exciting projects to do, allowed me to achieve success in my job, and has gifted me with outstanding relationships with friends and family. Moreover, I've become more mature, peaceful, and secure, which makes me grateful. That is worth more than any amount of money.

God liberated me from being desperate. I think I will marry one day, but even if that day never comes, I am at peace. No matter what, I'll be fine.

Reminder #2: Take Care of Your Soul

Just because you have not found your soulmate, and may not have gone on a date for a while, does not mean you are weird. You are normal. But, like all normal people, you probably have some unresolved issues, and I encourage you now, in your single season, to explore what these issues may be and seek a solution. Being single provides us with a precious advantage when it comes to resolving any unsettled manner: it is much easier to fix ourselves when we are alone or unattached. In other words, leverage your single status to work on your soul.

In the nineteenth century, lawyer and church elder Horatio Spafford penned a beautiful hymn entitled, "It Is Well With My Soul." Here are some of the song's lyrics:

When peace like a river, attendeth my way,
When sorrows like sea billows roll
Whatever my lot, thou hast taught me to say
It is well, it is well, with my soul

That's the question I want you to ask yourself: "Is it well with my soul?" Spafford's lyrics may strike you as being even more powerful if you understand the trauma he experienced before writing the song. He lost his son in the Great Chicago Fire, which also drove him to financial ruin and made him decide to move to Europe. Because of a last-minute business obligation, he sent his family on ahead of him. Their ship collided with another in the middle of the ocean and sank, killing his four daughters. And yet, despite all this tragedy, Spafford was able to appreciate God's grace and to find peace in his soul, as witnessed in his beautiful lyrics.

Taking care of your soul is well worth your time and energy. In our notoriously fast-paced existence, we must remember that despite whatever is going on in our exterior world, it is vital to take care of our inner being. But nurturing our souls requires sustained effort.

To help take care of myself, I developed the habit of journaling. Early in the morning before turning on my smartphone, and sometimes at night before going to bed, I spend a few minutes writing down my thoughts and feelings. I find journaling works best at times like these, when my busy life quiets down a bit because distraction is the worst enemy of taking care of my soul.

When I was seventeen, I went to Spain with my youth group. On the way home, we tried to cross France with only one stop at a gas station. Close to the border to Switzerland, the red warning light flashed, but we wanted to get into Switzerland before we filled up again, taking advantage of the cheaper gas, so we kept going. A few kilometers from the border, the engine sputtered and stopped. We had to pull over and wait for someone to help us get gas before we could continue. It was no fun standing in the breakdown lane of the interstate.

The same thing can happen to us if we don't take care of our souls: we can sputter and breakdown, losing sight of what is truly important in our lives. Leadership coach Robin Sharma, who has worked with many successful businesspeople and leaders, says too few of us take care of our inner world. He warns us not to leave our inner world—our soul—unattended but instead to develop a daily routine of self-care. I feel this is especially important during your season of singleness. Make sure you can say, "It is well with my soul."

Reminder #3: Put Your World in Order

The story of Adam I mentioned in Chapter 7 highlights an important point to consider. By giving a name to each animal, Adam brought order to the fauna of the earth and thus to his life. Once Adam had finished, God put him into a deep sleep, and when he woke up, Eve was standing in front of him. Adam uttered a whoop of joy:

> *This at last is bone of my bones and flesh of my flesh.*
>
> **—GENESIS 2:23**

Once Adam was ready, with his world in order, he did not have to work to find his soulmate. God put Eve into his life. Perhaps this means He keeps us waiting to find our spouse because He wants us to prepare first by bringing order into our inner and outer worlds.

My parents advise married couples and often speak to them about the importance of putting their relationships with their parents in order. They have seen many marriage problems caused by one of the spouses maintaining a too-close relationship with their parents. The Bible says:

> *Therefore a man shall leave his father and his mother and hold fast to his wife.*
>
> **—GENESIS 2:24**

In Western cultures, we are encouraged to leave our parents' homes and create a new home with our spouses. This only works if we also detach ourselves from the emotional bonds with our parents in preparation for bonding with our spouses.

Reflecting on your life, do you notice any areas you need to put in order? Consider working on them now, while you have the time and freedom of your single season.

Reminder #4: Tend Your Inner Garden

How do we put our inner world in order? What does that mean? I believe our inner being is like a personal garden that we must carefully tend to make it flourish. At my current home, a gardener does a fabulous job taking care of all the common areas and yards, weeding, trimming branches, cutting the grass, and watering everything, so it continues to grow. His dedicated work allows us to enjoy the beauty of the flora surrounding us. In the same way, our inner gardens require effort. Recalling the hymn by Horatio Spafford mentioned above, consider using its words to check on your inner garden by regularly asking yourself, "Is it well with my soul?" Do you feel under pressure, empty, irritable, or are you excited, full of energy, and encouraged? Taking good care of your soul is vital since you cannot be a good spouse unless your emotional garden is flourishing.

A counseling course teacher helped me identify something that nourishes my inner garden. She said, "David, you need to be in wide-open spaces," and suggested I make a habit of climbing tall buildings or mountains to enjoy the views. Fortunately, at the time, I lived in the Lake Geneva area with its mountain peaks and steep hills, so I could easily go for walks or rides on my bicycle. At my workplace located on the hillside overlooking the city and the lake, I was able to enjoy the breath-taking views of the surrounding snowcapped mountains. This lesson taught me the environment that I put myself in greatly impacts my inner well-being. I need open spaces to feed my soul.

We cannot leave the tending of our inner garden to chance. Instead, we need to be intentional about it, making it our priority. Apartheid activist and South African President Nelson Mandela understood this, often employing William Ernest Henley's quote, "I am the master of my fate, I am the captain of my soul." Despite suffering tremendous hardship during his twenty-seven years of imprisonment, Mandela deliberately took care of his inner being, thereby keeping his hopes alive, which allowed him to become the first black president of South Africa and abolished apartheid there. He accomplished great things because he continuously nurtured his soul.

If you want God to use you at your fullest potential, you have to protect your soul, too. Are there any toxic people around you who make you feel depressed? Do certain people in your life drain your energy? Have you been working too much lately? Does your busy and unhealthy lifestyle deplete you? We all need regular inner check-ups. Slow down and feel your soul. How do you feel when everything else quiets down? Do you notice any unrest, unease, lack of peace, fear, or sadness? Identify the cause of this stress and do your best to alleviate it.

Think about the changes you should make in your life to take better care of your soul. To get the best results, I encourage you to make a plan. When I prepare to participate in a marathon, I follow a strict protocol to keep my training on schedule. Likewise, I try to adhere to regular practices like journaling to keep my inner conditioning on track. Too often, we neglect our souls. Michael Pietrzak, a mindset and success coach, wrote, "The most neglected piece of any productivity plan is your most important asset: YOU." He encouraged his readers to "invest in self-care." In other words, do what you need to do to tend to your emotional garden.

Keeping a flower garden alive requires the right amount of water, sunlight, and nutrients. Our inner garden is no different. It also must be fed the correct elements in appropriate amounts. How do you feed your soul? What do you let in? For instance, consider the literature you have been reading recently. What messages do they convey? In many cities in Switzerland, free newspapers are available at places like bus stops and train stations. I used to browse through them in the morning on my way to work, but I stopped when I noticed the negative news and celebrity gossip made me feel frustrated, unsatisfied, and increased my craving to be in a relationship. I realized I was improperly feeding my soul.

Instead, I try to give my soul a treat by taking myself on soul-satisfying dates. For example, on a trip to Southeast Asia, I had a stopover in Bangkok. Since I was spending the entire weekend alone in the big metropolis, I decided to treat myself by going to a rooftop bar. Overlooking the vast city, I had a good time enjoying a delicious cocktail and feeding my soul.

Take care of yourself by finding places, people, and atmospheres that put you in a good mood. Your inner garden needs these moments to flourish and thrive.

Reminder #5: Becoming the Person You're Looking for Is Looking For

When I was a teenager, I would say: "Nobody is perfect; I'm nobody!" I thought this was funny. Now that I have grown more mature, instead of looking for the perfect woman, I've changed my focus, inspired in part by pastor Andy Stanley's teaching series, "The New Rules for Love, Sex & Dating." Dispelling the right-person myth, he said you should become the person who the person you are looking for is looking for. Such a statement was a game-changer for me since it took the focus off the other person and put it on me. In other words, it makes you focus on the only part of the relationship you can change: yourself, since you can't change the other person.

I find this to be a great way of looking at a relationship, too. As Jesus said, "It is more blessed to give than to receive" (Acts 20:35). By making myself a better person, I can become a blessing for my future wife. One evening in my church small group, we came up with the metaphor of making ourselves a gift for our future wife to unwrap—a beautiful way to imagine a relationship.

In his book, *The Compound Effect*, Darren Hardy writes that he made a list of all the attributes his future wife should have, coming up with forty different points. But then, instead of waiting and hoping to meet such a woman one day, he turned his list around and asked himself, "What do I need to do to become exactly that person?" He became the person he was looking for was looking for. In the end, he says, "I met that very person."

Reminder #6: Invest in Your Education

Once again, I emphasize that you can use this time while single to do whatever you want to do without regard for the dreams or needs of a spouse or family. If you choose, you may use your time to become a student again since you have a unique opportunity to perfect your talents. I read that now, in some fields, your college education becomes obsolete within five years of graduation, and therefore life-long learning has never been as important as it is today. Consider developing the habit of learning something new every day for at least thirty minutes.

Of course, this isn't a new concept. In the Bible, Paul recognized the value of continued education, making this request of his friend Timothy:

When you come, bring the cloak that I left with Carpus at Troas, also the books, and above all the parchments.

—2 TIMOTHY 4:13

Paul made it a priority to keep learning his entire life.

Like him, as singles, you and I have more time and energy to learn new skills. And since you don't yet have a family to feed, you probably have money left over at the end of the month. Because of these fortunate circumstances, I've decided to spend 10 percent of my time learning and spend 10 percent of my income on education. Although I sometimes have a difficult time justifying spending such a large percentage of my income on expenditures like books, subscriptions, conferences, and coaching, I realize the education I gain will benefit me for the rest of my life. More importantly, I can use my enhanced skills to assist others.

You may feel you don't have adequate time to devote to learning. Here comes my challenge to you: Add up how much screen time you use each week—the crazy number of hours you spend looking at your social media feed and swiping profiles on *Tinder*. Do this by recording all the times you open your social media app: five minutes at the bus stop, a half-hour on the train on the way to work, or an hour when you return home and are tired and want to give yourself a treat. Whenever it may be, record the amount of time spent online and then think about dedicating that time to pulling out a textbook instead of your smartphone. If you are not a book reader, consider using audiobooks. I do. Now while driving or waiting in line at a store, I listen to a book. Although it's only five minutes here and there, it has a massive impact on my life. Instead of spending my time surfing the internet, I'm learning something new that will benefit me, and I may use to help others.

I also encourage you to become curious and try out things you have never done before. Experiment with a new craft, learn to play a musical instrument, or travel to a place you've never seen before. If nothing else comes of it, at least you will have something fun and interesting to talk about on your next date. Maybe read some books about building healthy relationships. That way, instead of making the mistakes yourself, you get to painlessly learn from other people's experiences. You also could learn more by reading books on dating and marriage, talking to marriage counselors, and spending quality time with married friends. Ask them what they know. All of these activities will help you prepare for marriage. Why not learn what you can now? Chances are, the information will come in handy once you are in a relationship.

With better awareness, you can make better choices, and when you make better choices, you will see better results.

—ROBIN SHARMA, LEADERSHIP COACH

Many of my early serious relationships suffered because I didn't have the experience or knowledge to effectively navigate the waters of dating. If I had had more education in the fine art of relationships, I might have made wiser choices and had to endure fewer emotional struggles. Learning something new is always helpful and provides long-lasting benefits.

Reminder #7: Become a Single Influencer

When I started my blog, I chose the name "Singleinfluencer" because I wanted to influence the world and not allow anyone or any situation to talk me out of living my very best life. I intend to follow this path of purpose and live with high expectations.

Psychologist and author Dr. Benjamin Hardy once asked his readers, "What if you only had six months left to live?" encouraging them to think about their daily activities and whether or not they were pursuing their life goals. When I considered Dr. Hardy's question, I realized that many of my activities, like binging social media and watching non-relevant videos on *YouTube*, do not get me any closer to my goals. I asked myself, "How should I change my activities? What should I do instead?"

I also figured out that worrying about things wouldn't help since it also wasted time and energy. If I worry just twice a day for five minutes, it totals more than 600 hours in ten years. What a waste of a lot of time! So, what should I do with that time instead? I could listen to sixty audiobooks. Or meet with young people and teach them some skills they lack, or perhaps coach them to become better leaders. I could even serve four-hour shifts at my local charity for 150 afternoons. All of these options—and hundreds like them—would be far better uses of my time than worrying.

When we become singles living with purpose and on purpose, we can help make the world a better one. I suggest you decide now to become someone who lives your life and gives everything to accomplish your dreams.

CHAPTER 9: WRAP-UP

You may perceive your single season as a long waiting period. Surrendering your desire to meet your soulmate enables you to wait in peace and make the most of your singleness. It's your opportunity to take care of your inner well-being, thus becoming your better future self. Take good care of your soul, invest in yourself, and fulfill your purpose to make this world a better place. In short, become the person your future soulmate would love to find.

CHAPTER 9: TAKEAWAYS
WAITING IN PEACE

POINTS TO CONSIDER

1. Taking care of your inner being is vital. Looking after your soul is well worth your time and energy. A daily routine of self-care helps make this a priority.

2. As a single person, you have a significant advantage because it is much easier to resolve any unsettled matters when you are alone and unattached than in a relationship.

3. Your singleness is a gift, allowing you to become a better version of yourself. You have the opportunity to become the person that the person you are looking for is looking for. So, make learning a priority, work on correcting your flaws, and live your life to make a difference.

QUESTIONS FOR GROUPS

1. How do you take care of your emotional garden, your inner well-being?

2. Do you have any unsettled issues from a past relationship or any character traits you feel you should change? What could you do today to start the process?

3. How can you become the person that the person you are looking for is looking for?

ACTION STEPS TO TAKE

1. In your journal, make a list of attributes you are looking for in your life partner.

2. Ask yourself, "How do I need to change to become that person myself?"

3. Create a plan to become that better version of yourself and commit to it.

CHAPTER 10

MAKING TIME AND SPACE FOR LOVE

Take the first step in faith. You don't have to see the whole staircase, just take the first step.

—MARTIN LUTHER KING JR.,
MINISTER AND CIVIL RIGHTS LEADER

STORY OF A SINGLE

I was single for most of my thirties. I had a full life: a demanding job in the corporate world, dancing, church, and activities with my friends. Even though, in theory, I was open to another relationship, in reality, I wasn't ready. I had been hurt in the past, and I still needed to heal.

I began a personal journey to discover my purpose in life. As part of this, I took a three-month sabbatical to serve in a prison ministry in South Africa. When I arrived in Cape Town, I found my key contact was going on a Christian leadership conference and had signed me up to join her. At the conference, one of the speakers talked about the labels we carry. This helped me recognize I had been wearing a label saying I don't deserve a good Christian husband and family. Praying about it and asking God to heal my past hurts were important steps to my becoming open to a new relationship.

The year before I turned forty, I moved to a new city to take a senior management role. I joined a church where there were no other people my age with my type of job. For a while, I was in a long-distance relationship, but when that ended, I found myself praying, "I don't have time to actively look for a spouse. You've called me here to be in this job and to serve at this church. If it's in Your plan for me to get married, You'd better send someone." I didn't consciously decide to stay single, but I wasn't looking for a relationship either. I felt that God's purpose for my life was more important than whether I was going to be married or single for the rest of my life.

Not long after that conversation with God, a man named Daniel turned up for the first time at my church group. We got to know each other gradually at our weekly meetings. After a while, he offered to give me a lift home, and we would chat in the car. I thought he was a nice guy, but I was totally surprised when he asked me if I was interested in something more than a friendship. I was also extremely nervous because I didn't know if he was aware of how old I was. I told him upfront, "When you're a little older, and you're clear on what God's calling you to do, the only point in getting married is if you're going to be stronger for God's Kingdom together than as individuals." I wanted to make sure we started the relationship by sharing our callings and visions for life, and of course, I wanted him to know how old I was!

We began to date. Every Friday after work, Daniel would come and pick me up so we could have dinner together. On weekends, we often went on long hikes, talking the whole time. At church, we served together and were able to see each other interact with other people.

Daniel and I got married when I was forty-four. Getting married in your late thirties or forties is different. On the one hand, you know yourself pretty well and what's really important to you, which can be an advantage because clearly stated values and outlooks are so vital to a healthy marriage. But, on the other hand, marrying later in life means you have already acquired a lot of habits and routines and may need to let some of them go to allow space for your future spouse.

—RUTH, FIFTY-THREE YEARS OLD, SWITZERLAND

By this point in your life, you probably have discovered your purpose. You've found something you want to do, and you feel you are making a valuable contribution to others by doing it. But now that you've made a life without a spouse, what will happen if you meet your soulmate? How will you adapt to being part of a couple? In the next two chapters, we will explore the transition to a relational season.

MOSES: MAKING TIME AND SPACE FOR LOVE

Let us begin by looking at Moses's story in the Book of Exodus and see how he made time and space for love. Moses was a long-term single. We don't know why because the Bible tells us little about his life in Pharaoh's palace. Knowing the culture, however, we may assume he had the opportunity to find his wife there, and yet Moses remained unmarried. His companions must have rolled their eyes and asked, "You are forty and still single?" But even though he grew up in the palace and dressed like an Egyptian, Moses was a Hebrew. He honored the God of his ancestors, Abraham, Isaac, and Jacob, and might have yearned for a soulmate who believed in Yahweh, too. Or perhaps he simply enjoyed the freedom he had as a single man amidst a court full of beautiful women.

One day, while taking a walk, Moses enjoyed listening to the conversation of two other Hebrew men. He wondered if they realized he was one of their brothers. An Egyptian supervisor appeared, yelled at the two men, and struck them. Moses retaliated by hitting the Egyptian so hard he killed him. When Pharaoh heard what his protégé had done, Moses had to flee to a country far away.

In that country, Moses met a charming woman named Zephora at a well. He stood up for her when shepherds tried to chase her and her sisters away. Her father thanked Moses for his bravery and offered him Zephora's hand in marriage—the beginning of a beautiful love story.

Although Moses lived a life of luxury at Pharaoh's palace, he had to leave Egypt and travel to a distant country before he was ready for marriage. Once he was in his new home, however, Moses felt he was ready for a new relationship season.

Like Moses, you may need to prepare yourself for a relationship. It may be that you are too busy or too afraid to give up the freedom you are enjoying in your single season. What obstacles do you see in your life that might prevent you from embracing a new relationship?

Last Christmas, I was excited to have my brother and his family visit me. I had moved to Cambodia a few months before and was looking forward to spending Christmas with some of my family. I greatly enjoyed hanging out with my four-year-old nephew but quickly became aware of how much attention is required by a young child. I thought, "Oh wow, family life is exhausting!" I was no longer positive I wanted to get married and have kids. My bachelor life suddenly seemed so much simpler and less complicated.

DECIDING TO MAKE ROOM FOR A RELATIONSHIP

If you are like me, when you were younger, you were probably careful to allow time and space for a possible relationship. You wanted to be sure if the right person showed up at your door, you'd be ready to enter into a committed relationship with them right away, even if it meant you had to make big changes, such as moving to a different town. You were focused on finding your soulmate.

But now that you and I are older, we've moved onto a different phase of our lives and are more focused on other things like our careers or service to God. We've settled into comfortable lifestyles that don't automatically include space for a spouse or children, as my Christmas experience with my brother and his son demonstrated to me. I realized I still wanted some aspects of being married and having a family but wanted to skip the less savory parts, like dealing with an active toddler. In short, I wanted to cherry-pick the advantages of being married and leave problematic aspects aside.

In recent years, I have decided to put God's Kingdom first, no matter the cost. My move to Cambodia was an all-in decision. I knew when I quit my job and sold my belongings, I was limiting my options. Now, if I met the woman of my dreams on an airplane, I might have to abandon my commitment to Cambodia and follow her to the country she calls home. To welcome someone to share my life with me now, I must be prepared to give up some of my current freedoms and be willing to adjust my habits to accommodate her. It is not that I no longer want to be married—I simply need to deliberately create time and space for a future spouse.

MAKING TIME AND SPACE FOR LOVE IS EASIER SAID THAN DONE

I have become content with many aspects of my flexible lifestyle as a single. For one thing, I can travel wherever and whenever I want. Except for my boss, I have no one else to consider when making plans. I buy my airline ticket; change into my preferred outfit of T-shirt, shorts, and flip-flops; and then go. I enjoy these freedoms.

We appreciate many comfortable habits when we live alone. You may feel that there is no need to change these habits, or perhaps you are fearful that you will resent having to change them to accommodate someone else. Regardless of the reason, if you want to have a committed relationship with someone, you must lay aside your selfishness and take up the challenge to change. You must say, "No," to living the single life, which may be difficult.

Have I filled up my life too much and have no room left for a relationship? Have I adopted a selfish attitude? If I date someone, I think, "I'm busy doing important things at church and work—I'm trying to change the world—so you need to adjust to suit my lifestyle." Allowing room for a serious relationship would mean cutting back on some of the things I do now, which would be a tough decision for me to make.

Do you have a lifestyle you would have to change if you became involved with someone? Are you willing to make those changes? Would they be difficult for you?

FINDING A BALANCE

Throughout this book, I have urged you to live your single life to its fullest by identifying a mission or project you feel passionate about and then totally committing yourself to it. I believe this is the way for us to thrive as singles while we wait for our prince or princess to arrive. However, there is a caveat to this advice: pursue your passion but continue to allow room in your life for the possibility of a relationship. In other words, maintain a balance between your current life and your hopes for your future.

I have always been committed and passionate about whatever I do. When I have a project with a purpose that is bigger than myself, I often spend hour after hour working on it with no regard for anything else. For example, at my church in Lausanne, I volunteered to write and print pamphlets to use when teaching small groups. I remember one particular evening I was working hard, researching a topic and designing a beautiful flyer. I looked at my watch and found that it was after midnight. I realized that I had allowed myself to lose balance in my life. A few years later, when I agreed to head up our church's video team, I thought I had resolved the issue of priorities and would be able to maintain a healthy balance with my time. Needless to say, I was wrong and my new project overwhelmed me. I spent so much time editing the videos for the team, it was like I was working a second job. If my soulmate had shown up at that time, I probably wouldn't have even noticed she was there, let alone have been able to spend time with her.

How can I meet my soulmate if I am such an overachiever? My Cambodian friends would say, "Cannot, sir!" and they would be correct. I need to find a balance in my life. So do you. We all need to live our single life with purpose, commitment, and passion, but, at the same time, we need to maintain available space in which a relationship can occur. If there is no space and time available for such a relationship, it will not happen. According to science, it takes at least sixty-six days to establish a new routine. It is not an overnight thing. So, starting now, make a habit of allowing space in your life for your soulmate. In a few months, you may see results.

Once you learn to live your life with balance, several things will happen. First of all, you will find you are more relaxed around others because you have allowed time and space in your life for them. Secondly, others will notice that you are available to them and will appreciate this. When I met a single professor, I was attracted to her, and I sensed she liked me, too. At the same time, I realized that she led an extremely busy life with very little time available to spend with me. For me to see her, I would have had to constantly revise my plans to accommodate her crazy work schedule. It may not come as a surprise to you that I was not thrilled with this arrangement and, in the end, decided not to pursue a dating relationship with her.

Now that I'm over forty, I find I'm less flexible regarding my schedule and habits. Also, my responsibilities at work have increased, I've taken on important projects at church, and I've started to develop new sources of income. All of these commitments take time and require planning, especially if I want to leave room in my life for love. Finding a balance in my life must be a priority.

DEVELOPING AN OPEN MIND

Take a minute to picture your ideal spouse. What does he look like? What does she do for work? What is his personality like? Now, consider how focused you are on finding exactly that person. Are you open to possibilities or intent on locating someone who precisely meets your criteria?

In the past, I have made a list of the qualities I would like to see in my future spouse and have then wondered if that was a good idea.

On the one hand, I may be able to use my list to help me recognize my soulmate when I meet her. On the other hand, if I exclusively look for someone who satisfies all the requirements on my list, I may miss someone different who would have been a great spouse. In other words, the list may increase the chance of me becoming narrow-minded about my princess selection.

Dr. Benjamin Hardy's thoughts challenged me to do a gut check:

Because people have an idea of a fixed and innate personality, they spend loads of time looking for the "perfect" person to date and marry. Many people never commit to long-term relationships because of this fundamental misunderstanding about people. They think that when they find that "right" person, everything will just work out. This is ignorance.

Creating a successful marriage or partnership is just as difficult, and just as rewarding, as parenting. Just as you will never "find" yourself, you will never "find" that perfect soul mate. The reason people want to find that perfect person, just like they want to find that perfect job, is because the "discovery" perspective is selfish. The end goal is all about meeting your own gratifications and happiness rather than happiness being the by-product of something much bigger.

Rather than marrying a person for who they currently are, it takes far more wisdom and discernment to marry for who you can see them becoming—their future self—and how they will enable you to become your desired future self. Will marrying this person enable you to do and be all that you truly want? And will you enable them to be all that they truly want? Who and what could both of you become if you were partners? Developing a powerful relationship isn't about "finding," but collaboratively creating and becoming new people together, through the relationship.[4]

---

4   Benjamin Hardy, "Personality Isn't Permanent: Break Free from Self-Limiting Beliefs and Rewrite Your Story," (Portfolio, 2020)

Making a list of the characteristics I was looking for in my soul-mate helped me to understand what was important to me. It also led me to fall into the trap of looking for the perfect person to date. As we have explored in previous chapters, don't focus on meeting the right person. Instead, become the right person by improving yourself. And, if you have written a list of attributes you want to find in your soul-mate, look beyond it and consider other possibilities. A friend once told me that he never wanted to marry an older woman. Then he met one, and they were friends for a while when he had an eye-opening moment, realizing that her age was not all that important to him. "Soon after, I asked her out. And not long after that, we were married."

Develop an open mind. You never know what great things can happen.

ALLOWING OPPORTUNITIES BY TAKING RISKS

After my last relationship failure, I didn't want to experience the pain and loss of a breakup again, so I prayed to God, "Next time, please stop me from pursuing a woman if she is not the right one for me. If she is not Your choice, close the door." I was looking for a way to date without risking possible heartbreak. What I didn't realize was that my risk-avoidance strategy prevented me from falling in love.

Since my last relationship, I have become a pro at the keeping-it-safe game. Whenever I feel the slightest pang of tender emotions, I carefully control them in an attempt to protect myself. Using my analytical brain—developed during years of study and research—I rationalize, "This relationship will not work because of XX, and if you do YY, you'll end up in ZZ. Oh, did I mention the option AA? Watch out.

It can lead you to BB and then to ZZ." I come up with reason after reason why the relationship will fail, and then, because of my poor attitude, it does fail. No surprise there. Rather than taking a chance on the relationship and seeing where it goes naturally, I talk myself out of it by overthinking it. Merriam-Webster defines "overthinking" this way: "to put too much time into thinking about or analyzing (something) in a way that is more harmful than helpful." When it comes to dating, such overthinking certainly causes more harm than good and has destroyed many potentially good relationships.

Yes, it is wise to think before you jump into a relationship. However, you must realize that entering a relationship is a risky business. There are no guarantees in the world of dating. My prayer to God after my last breakup was an attempt to avoid the dangers of dating, but if I am not willing to take risks, I will never manage to build a meaningful relationship with a woman. I have to accept the fact that I cannot predict whether a relationship will succeed or not. That's Alice-in-Wonderland thinking. Real life is much messier and more unpredictable. You and I cannot play it safe. Instead, we need to put ourselves out there, take risks, and strive for the best possible outcome.

WAITING FOR GOD'S TIME

Only God can give you the love you're looking for, and only God can give you the person that loves Him enough to deserve you.

—UNKNOWN

You and I can prepare ourselves and make space in our lives for love, but then we must rely on God to send the right person in our direction. The challenge with this is that God has different timing than we do. I want a relationship now. If it is not going to happen now, I'd like to know when it will happen so I may prepare for it. But God does things in His own time, requiring me to trust that He will not forget about me and that He is working behind the scenes to fulfill my dreams. Also, I do not want just any relationship; I have high expectations. When will God give me the love I am looking for? I will try my best to be open-minded and flexible about my list of spousal requirements, but I'd like to know that He is at least considering my requests and would appreciate a timeline showing me when my soulmate is coming.

Throughout history, people have come up with a variety of theories about time. A writer named *Wolf* on *Yahoo Answers* offered this explanation of the difference between the concepts of Kairos and Chronos, which was edited by Kingdom Shifts on kairosmomentum.com:

The ancient Greeks had two words for time: Chronos and Kairos. Chronos refers to chronological or sequential time. The clock and calendar measure Chronos time. It is orderly, rhythmic, and predictable. It is what we moderns typically think of as time. Kairos time, on the other hand, has a more nebulous meaning. It does not have an equivalent word in English. The least descriptive translation would be "in-between time"—a moment of undetermined time in which something extraordinary happens.

God works in His own dimension, not following the idea of Chronos. He knows the best possible time to bring me the person I am looking for—His Kairos—when "something special happens."

My friend, Annie, who you read about in Chapter 7, told me she felt God had neglected her, so she called Him out on it, "Did you forget, Lord, that I want to meet someone?"

God answered her, "Wait, and you'll see what I have in store for you."

Looking back years later, as a wife and mom, she concluded, "God's timing was perfect. He sent me a husband who has the values and the character I asked for and shares a similar sense of purpose. Even though I was thirty-nine years old at the time, we had no trouble having a child together."

If you wait, you will get what God wants to give you, which will be a far more abundant gift than whatever you may have requested or expected. Just know that this gift will be delivered according to God's Kairos, not your own Chronos. Be patient.

CHAPTER 10: WRAP-UP

Waiting on God's timing is important, as is making space in our lives for love. Now that you have laid these foundations, you are ready for the next step: dating. As John Paul Young's hit song from the 1970s said, "Love is in the air."

CHAPTER 10: TAKEAWAYS

MAKING TIME AND SPACE FOR LOVE

POINTS TO CONSIDER

1. You develop many comfortable living habits while single. If you want to welcome someone to share your life, you have to give up certain freedoms and change some habits.

2. As you grow older, you tend to settle into a comfortable lifestyle that doesn't automatically include space for a spouse or children.

3. Overthinking may hinder you from dating. Remember, there is no risk-free relationship, and so it's impossible to play it safe. Instead, when God opens a door for you, take it. Accept the risk and strive to achieve the best possible outcome.

QUESTIONS FOR GROUPS

1. What freedoms do you enjoy most as a single?

2. Which of these freedoms will be the most difficult for you to let go upon entering a relationship?

3.   Are you prepared to take the inherent risks in committing to a relationship?

ACTION STEPS TO TAKE

1.   Write a list of the freedoms you feel you may need to give up when you enter a committed relationship.

2.   Write down what you will gain by surrendering each of those freedoms.

CHAPTER 11

DATING

A lot of the heartache and confusion we feel
in dating stems from treating dating mainly as
practice for marriage (clarity through intimacy),
instead of as discernment toward marriage
(clarity and then intimacy).

—MARSHALL SEGAL, MANAGING EDITOR OF DESIRINGGOD.ORG

STORY OF A SINGLE

Before I surrendered my life to Jesus, I had a few relationships in which I had a lot of fun. But in reality, they were not fun. The more I tried to check the boxes on my to-do-before-growing-old-and-getting-married list, the worse I felt. Sex never made me feel ashamed or dirty, and I thought it was fun, but when the fun was over, my heart felt empty, like someone had stolen a piece of it.

Now that I know Jesus, my life has turned around. I let Him pour His love into my wounds and fill the hole in my heart so that I now feel loved. God has changed the way I look at dating, too. I believe living a love story with Him will open the way for the love story with my soulmate. Prayer now plays a pivotal role in my dating life. Soon after becoming a Christian, I prayed my first prayer, asking God if I should date a guy I found attractive. Two hours later, the guy left and never talked to me again—God's answer to my prayer.

I must admit, before I found God, dating was easier. If I like dancing, I'd go dancing, and I'd meet a dancer. Now that I am a Christian, finding someone who enjoys dancing or mountain biking is only one part of the equation. Now, he has to be a Christian, too. I tried a Christian dating site but found it creepy. Since that didn't work for me, I asked my church leader if we could set up a singles party or group to help singles meet other singles. I know there's no guarantee that I'd meet someone special at such a gathering, but if I don't make an effort, I know nothing will happen. Even if I don't meet my soulmate, perhaps I might meet someone who knows a special guy.

Recently, I told a friend about being single and unhappy. She said, "I know someone who's about your age, and I think the two of you might hit it off." Her friend turned out to be a nice, Christian guy, and we went on some enjoyable dates together. Although we didn't end up in a long-term relationship, God blessed me by being close to me. My love for God surpassed my disappointment with the relationship.

The story of a now-married pastor who went on a mission trip to Brazil encouraged me. His now-wife traveled nearby on a different boat. Because of technical problems, both ships had to stop at an island in the middle of the ocean. That's how the pastor and his wife met.

Hopefully, boats will stop at an island for my husband and me, too. Nothing is impossible for God.

—CÉLINE,* 31 YEARS OLD, FRANCE

*Identity changed

Like Jennifer, when I go on dates, I want to spend time doing activities we both enjoy. As a Christian, I believe it also is important for me to date someone who shares my core values and beliefs. In this way, I feel we will match each other more completely.

A friend of mine told me about a guy she dated for five years. He was very kind, got along well with her friends and family, and they had fun together hiking and going to music concerts. But the guy was often drunk and used illegal drugs, which greatly upset my friend. When he refused to stop, she broke up with him, even though she loved him very much. They had many shared interests but did not agree on some core values.

MY SOULMATE CHECKLIST

I thought it might be helpful to share my list of the attributes I am looking for in my soulmate. Although I understand that I may not find someone who meets all of these criteria, writing this list helped me discover what I truly value in a person, whether that person is my future spouse, a friend, or even myself. Perhaps this list may help you realize what is important to you, too.

Attribute #1: Values

First and foremost, I am looking for someone who shares my core values. I want these values to become the basis upon which our relationship is built. If my future spouse and I have different values, we may not recognize this as a problem at first. However, as our relationship evolves, these differences would gain more significance, especially when we begin to educate our children. Which set of values would we teach them? Hers or mine? How would we choose? If your fundamental values are incongruent with your spouse's, your family will suffer.

For this reason, I feel it is important that you do not compromise on your fundamental values but instead find someone who shares them with you.

My Christian faith is one of my core values. I want to seek God's Kingdom first and would like to marry a woman who wants to do this, too. As President Abraham Lincoln said, "A house divided against itself cannot stand." For my spouse and me to stand together as a couple, a shared faith is paramount.

I value generosity and charity, too. Although I might enjoy owning expensive clothes, a fancy car, or a large house, I would much rather spend my money in other ways. I make sure to take care of my needs, but then use my extra income to help others. I believe this is what God calls me to do. I would like to find a wife who shares my passion for generosity.

Values lay the foundation of a relationship. Take the time to identify your core values. Then share them upfront when you date someone. If you find you both have the same fundamental values, they might form the basis of a solid relationship.

Attribute #2: Chemistry

The next thing I look for with a prospective spouse is chemistry: the emotion two people experience when they share a special connection. In other words, I want us both to feel good when we spend time together. One day, I met a great woman of God. She served in her church and was influential in the business world. I felt we had many core values in common and so I checked off the "values" box on my soulmate checklist right away. But when I was with her and her friends, sometimes I felt uncomfortable, as if I couldn't be myself. She had a strong personality and strong opinions, and I felt the need to change to fit into her life. I saw a red warning flag telling me our relationship lacked chemistry. We did not share a binding connection, and I did not feel at peace in her company.

Listen to your heart and gut. They are often right about chemistry. I believe spouses should be best friends, too. Being friends is about feeling comfortable with each other and having the freedom to say anything without fear of being judged. Spouses are friends with chemistry.

Attribute #3: Intellect

Although physical attraction is essential to any long-term relationship—more on that in Attribute #5—what makes it last is the capability to share thoughts and ideas with someone at a similar intellectual level as yourself. If your intellects are well-matched, you also can have meaningful conversations and solve conflicts with your partner. How boring it would be to spend time with someone you couldn't talk to. And how difficult it would be to build a relationship with someone you don't understand.

I'm a thinker and like to share my latest thoughts and ideas. I don't necessarily expect my wife to understand the projects I do at work, but I need to be with someone who can follow my thinking and challenge my ideas. When I was younger, I would not have thought to list "intellect" as a criterion on my soulmate checklist because I didn't understand its importance. As leadership coach Robin Sharma says, "With better awareness, you make better choices, and you get better results." Now that I'm older, I understand the need to be able to relate intellectually with my future mate and so seek this quality in her.

Attribute #4: Common Hobbies

I am an outdoor sports guy. Running, cycling, swimming, beach-volley, and skiing are just a few of the many activities I enjoy. But when I returned home with Lauren, my new girlfriend from the church camp in Spain, I discovered she disliked participating in outdoor sports—all of them. The only physical activity we were able to do together was walking around the block, which I found somewhat boring. At the beginning of our relationship, this was no big deal. After a while, though, I mourned our lack of common hobbies.

According to Gary Chapman's book, *The Five Love Languages*, my first love language is quality time, which explains why I soon became frustrated with my relationship with Lauren. Not only could I not share my outdoor activities with her, but she also showed little interest in them. I remember one day I returned from snowboarding in the nearby mountains, excited about the fantastic powder we'd found, and she had no idea what I was talking about and couldn't have cared less. This inability to share quality time participating in common hobbies was one of the main reasons we eventually broke up.

Everyone has their own interests and tastes, so it would be unrealistic to expect spouses to share all the same hobbies. In fact, it probably wouldn't be healthy to spend that much time together. However, having one or two hobbies in common allows the couple to share quality time, create memories, and thus strengthening their relationship.

Attribute #5: Physical Attraction

In the conservative church environment where I grew up, I heard little about the importance of physical attraction, and when someone did address the topic, it was combined with words of caution, such as: "Beware of temptation." "Outward beauty is shallow; inward beauty is more important." "God looks at someone's heart." "In time, beauty will vanish." Although those statements may be valid in the right context, physical attraction is a natural and necessary part of a spousal relationship.

In the past, I focused too much on a woman's outward appearance. I thought if she were pretty, tall, and graceful, I'd hit the girlfriend jackpot and had found the perfect person to date. Today, I am convinced that a person's inner beauty reveals itself as outward beauty, which is why I pay more attention to things like a woman's values, chemistry, and intellect. However, when I meet a woman, I still do look at how she dresses, how her eyes shine, and how she moves. After all, how someone looks says a lot about her. Physical attraction is essential. If you don't feel any butterflies in your stomach when you are looking at the other person, something is lacking.

CREATIVE WAYS TO MEET NEW PEOPLE

Being single is great. But for most of us, it will not last forever. Isn't that good news? Counting on God's guidance and waiting for his timing is important. And yet, we must do our part, too. When it comes to finding your significant other, there are spiritual and practical components to consider.

Below you will find suggestions of creative ways to meet your soulmate. If one way doesn't work for you, another might, so keep trying. And remember God will be right there with you, every step of the way.

Method #1: Consider Online Dating

Online dating provides single people with a substantially higher chance of success in finding a partner. Rather than being limited to the singles living in your immediate area, you can now reach out to people all over the globe. When I understood the fantastic potential of online dating sites, I signed up. I was wary at first and entered the sites cautiously, but then found myself enjoying the dopamine kick of browsing through the profiles. In the beginning, the sheer number of potential women I could reach out to overwhelmed me, so I had to learn to focus on just a few at a time.

Online dating can be a powerful tool, and I encourage you to use it—with one warning: if you are not careful, it can consume much of your time and energy. To maintain a balance in my life, I developed the discipline of visiting the sites for predetermined lengths of time and focusing on two to three women only.

I have found online dating challenging. I tried it for several years and met some great women but found that some of the restrictions of this method of meeting women made me uncomfortable. On many of the sites, after the second or third date, I felt I had to choose whether or not to limit my contact with her. In a face-to-face setting, I like to allow a relationship to progress more organically by maintaining a level of friendship until the magic moment hits … or doesn't.

For example, I enjoyed my first date with one of the women I met, but after the second date, I grew unsure, sensing a lack of chemistry. She admitted she also was thinking about quitting. Nonetheless, we decided to try a third date, and then a fourth one, but despite her extraordinary qualities and the meaningful discussions we had, I never experienced a "Wow!" moment with her. We decided to meet yet another time, and that's when I began to feel the pressure to commit to an exclusive relationship with her. We had progressed into the undefined space between friends and there-might-be-more, and I didn't want to give her any false impressions about my feelings, so I broke off our relationship and decided to rethink online dating.

For me, online dating was difficult because of its lack of in-person contact and the pressure I felt to decide on the future of the relationship immediately. However, if you are comfortable deciding about a relationship after just a few dates, then online dating may be a powerful tool for you to use to find your soulmate.

Method #2: Ask Friends for Referrals

Everyday interactions with friends can lead to you meeting a new person who might become your future spouse. I am very grateful to my friends who have put me into contact with other singles. And I often meet single people while attending events such as birthday parties, BBQs, and weddings. This may not sound like a revolutionary idea, but if you are strategic about pushing yourself to get to know a new person at each event, you will be amazed at how quickly you can expand your circle of acquaintances, even if you only meet one new person each time. Challenge yourself to do it.

Also, like with professional networking, consider asking your friends if they know someone you should get to know. You'll be surprised to find nearly all of them do. Utilize these referrals to expand your network of friends and increase your chances of meeting someone special. Even if you do not meet your soulmate, the process will bolster your confidence so that when you do meet that special someone, you will have the courage to talk to them. So get up, switch off your Netflix series, and call a friend for a referral.

Method #3: Attend Christian Singles Hangouts

Thank you so much to each of you who organizes any kind of hangouts where singles can meet. In Lausanne, Switzerland, several churches have single communities, which they open to a variety of people, including those from other churches. They organize hangouts where they invite a diverse group of singles and provide a safe place for them to meet. These hangouts are great places to meet singles who share your values and commitment to helping others. Look for events like these near you.

Method #4: Join a Facebook Group

I wish I had known about Facebook groups earlier. I certainly would have joined one. I only discovered their potential recently as I was researching the content for this book. Facebook groups provide a safe forum for singles to meet, share ideas, and have intellectual discussions. They also allowed me to posit ideas for this book by posting some of my quotes and blog articles. "Facebook groups could be an alternative to online dating platforms," I thought. Or at least the groups could complement online dating. To find a great selection of exciting groups, type "Christian singles groups on Facebook" or "Christian singles groups near me" into the Facebook search bar.

Method #5: Serve in a New Ministry

"Where do the great Christian women hide?" I wondered. And then I got it: they are serving at church. If you aren't yet involved in your church, think about joining a group or two there. If you already do participate in your church community, consider switching over to a new ministry. If you happen to meet your future husband or wife that way—bingo! Chances are they will espouse similar core values to yours. And working together in a ministry is so much better than a date since you'll get to observe your potential Prince or Princess Charming in action with other people. Gentlemen, this means you get to meet your dear Mrs. Betterhalf in a setting without feeling any pressure. However, I must warn you: if finding your soulmate is your only motivation to serve in a new ministry at your church or charity organization, your chances of meeting him or her will decrease since folks will figure out you are only trolling for a date.

Even though I was not ready and not looking for a girlfriend, once when I was serving on a worship team at my church, I did meet a very special woman. We got to know each other well by meeting every week. We had fun together and had many occasions to see how we each reacted under stress as we dealt with conflicts and disappointments related to the worship team. Under different circumstances, I probably would have pursued a relationship with this woman. Serving alongside a person you find attractive is one of the best ways to get to know each other.

Method #6: Live for a Cause

Living for a cause makes you more attractive and is another great way to meet someone who shares your values. Author, counselor, and Christian lecturer John Eldridge wrote, "In the heart of every man is a desperate desire for a battle to fight, an adventure to live, and [someone] to rescue." In other words, we all want to live for a cause we feel is worthy of pursuing be part of an adventure. And that is why living for a cause makes you more attractive. Who wouldn't want to join you on the adventure of your lifetime?

Method #7: Go on a Mission Trip

I have been on two mission trips and feel they provided me with ideal opportunities to meet a potential future spouse. On my trips, I did not end up in a relationship, yet I was able to see the team members in a more profound way than simply being with them in a camp. We were together to accomplish a specific mission. All the members had to undergo a selection process since not everybody is ready to sacrifice a well-earned vacation to serve overseas. The people who participated tended to have a higher level of personal commitment that I felt was similar to my degree of dedication.

Whether you are in a big or small church, you can sign up for a mission trip with an organization that interests you. Why not giving it a try? Even if you do not find your soulmate, you will help others and have an experience you will never forget.

Method #8: Talk to a Stranger

On a business trip to San Francisco, I went out for dinner in a Mexican restaurant. As I was reading a book, waiting for my food to arrive, I spotted a woman sitting alone at the end of the bar and thought, "Why don't I invite her to sit with me?" figuring she might be on a business trip and feeling lonely, too. I introduced myself to her, asked her to join me, and then returned to my table, unsure whether or not she would accept my invitation. She did, saying my generous offer had moved her. We enjoyed a captivating conversation along with our meals.

I seldom talked to strangers, but after that encounter, I resolved to do it more. You never know what doors these random conversations can open. The stranger you are talking to may introduce you to one of their friends who becomes your future spouse. Or perhaps one day you write your most beautiful love story with the person you met at a Mexican restaurant in the Bay Area. Who knows?

Method #9: Try Virtual Dating

Even before COVID-19, the internet was impacting how we think about dating. Is it possible to have meaningful and satisfactory exchanges with other singles online? When you undergo a lockdown—such as the ones caused by the COVID crisis—you have no other choice. In many countries, we had to become creative and use technology to meet other singles. It was not my favorite method of meeting women, but it did work. The physical distance forced me to get to know the person on the screen in a meaningful way, through text and video chats. And it took the focus off the physical aspects of the relationship. Although it may not have been as personal as I would have liked, I did enjoy meeting other singles over the internet and appreciated the freedom it provided to reach out to anyone anywhere in the world.

All of the methods of meeting others mentioned above do not guarantee success. They may help you to meet someone, or they may not. If the time is not right, it won't happen, and that's fine. We have to remind ourselves that we cannot push our destiny. God is in control, and He is doing an excellent job at it.

TIPS FOR GETTING TO KNOW SOMEONE

Okay. Let's say that you've met someone you think might be "the one." What do you do next? How do you become better acquainted with that person to determine if he or she might be your soulmate? Below, I've listed some tips I use myself when trying to get to know someone better.

Tip #1: Take Your Time

You have been waiting for so long, and now you finally meet a potential spouse. All sorts of happy hormones—like dopamine and adrenaline—enter your bloodstream, make your mind go crazy, and encourage you to rush into the relationship. Only after the fact do you realize that might not have been the best way to deal with the situation.

Once I decide to ask someone out, I feel as if I have a gun pointed at my head. I fear if I don't move quickly enough, some other guy will ask her out first. Rather than approaching the woman calmly and gradually getting to know her, I'm inclined to pull out all the stops and barrage her with everything I can think of to impress her and make her interested in me. Thank God for my friends, who calm me down and encourage me to take my time and act more reasonably.

When getting to know someone new, taking your time is essential. A friend once told me that if the girl is the right one, she will wait patiently. This means there is no need to rush. My advice to you is to wait.

If you get the opportunity to go on a date with a special person, by all means, go and enjoy every minute of it. Let your feelings flow. Just don't rush it. Instead, remember that a relationship is more of a marathon than a sprint. Start slow and pace yourself. If the relationship is meant to be, you will eventually reach the finish line of marriage. In the meantime, however, you must protect your heart and the heart of your potential better half by gradually getting to know each other and ensuring that you truly are compatible. Otherwise, you may rush the relationship only to experience the heartbreak of discovering it is irreparably flawed in some way.

Keep your heart with all vigilance, for from it flow the springs of life.

—PROVERBS 4:23

If you want to thrive in life, you need to protect your heart since all creativity, energy, joy, determination, and perseverance flow from it. Trust your heart. Listen to it. Give it time to determine if your date is truly your soulmate. If the relationship is making you feel rushed or anxious, consider the reasons for this. If your date is putting pressure on you to hurry into something, that might be a red flag.

Tip #2: Meet in Different Settings

When you take your time with a relationship, you will have the opportunity to go out on several dates together. And if you are strategic, you should consider suggesting to meet in a variety of settings. By experiencing your relationship in different places, you will be able to see it from different perspectives.

I had a series of dates with a wonderful woman who lived in the Swiss-German part of Switzerland. For our dates, though, I brought her into my French-speaking culture to see how she handled being in an environment where she had to speak a different language. We also experimented with getting to know each other while enjoying different activities. We went ice skating, played badminton, went for a nice dinner in a restaurant, walked through a beautiful park, and went skiing. One evening, I even invited her to my apartment, where I cooked her a meal traditional to my region. I enjoyed getting to know her in these various environments because they allowed me to get a complete picture of her personality. And I found it took the focus off of the awkward newness of dating each other. It felt more like having a good friend instead of thinking "relationship" all the time.

By arranging dates in different settings, you will be able to view your potential soulmate from a variety of perspectives. This will also show you how he or she may react to different situations you may encounter later in your married life together.

Tip #3: Introduce Them to Your Friends

If you have the opportunity and you feel comfortable, try to introduce your date to your friends early on in your relationship. You can do this overtly by simply stating that you want them to meet each other, or you can do it undercover, by arranging for them to be in the same place at the same time, unbeknownst to your date.

I suggest that you introduce your date to your friends for two significant reasons. First, you can observe how your date interacts with your friends. Does he smile? Does she show genuine interest in your friends? Are there superficial signs? This is information that will help you assess the relationship. Secondly, after the date, you can ask your friends what they thought of her. I find this valuable. My friends know me well, and they can view my new relationship more objectively than I, so I want to know their opinions. They help me see things I might have missed and achieve more clarity in areas where I'm unsure. Of course, I do not rely exclusively on my friends' impressions but rather use their opinions to confirm mine. I am still the one who makes the final decision.

One thing I learned through experience: at the beginning of a relationship, I only let my best friends know that I'm dating someone. Otherwise, if my extended friend circle knows about my new girlfriend, I feel pressured by their expectations. Instead, I want to avoid their difficult questions and be able to decide on my own whether or not I want to pursue a serious relationship with her.

Tip #4: Speak Honestly about the Relationship

While you are dating, make sure to provide each other with updates on how each of you sees the relationship progressing. This will help you understand each other's feelings and will allow you to know what to expect from the relationship in the future. Talking openly like this may seem unromantic. After all, aren't you supposed to just experience the relationship and see where it goes? In fact, clear communication is one of the best methods for drawing a relationship closer.

On a one-day stopover, I met a woman with whom I had an exciting discussion about charities. After I returned home, she and I texted back and forth. One message became two, two became four, and not long after we had our first video call. I decided to fly over to spend a week together to find out if the relationship was worth pursuing. I was a bit hesitant, knowing one week can be a long time. Before I traveled, we clearly defined our intentions for the visit to avoid any disappointments caused by misaligned expectations. And then, during the week, we gave each other regular updates on how we were feeling about the relationship. From the beginning, we had transparent discussions. There were no false expectations.

If you begin a relationship by being open with each other about your expectations, wants, and needs, the relationship will be based upon an honest sharing of feelings and thoughts. And as sixteenth-century politician Edwin Sandys said, "Honesty is the best policy."

Tip #5: Pray Together

Sharing faith is the foundation of a relationship, and if you can establish this habit early on, it will strengthen the bond you share. Praying together can also help you make better decisions and achieve a feeling of spiritual compatibility. If you feel comfortable praying together before going out, do it. If it seems odd to you or your date, don't push it.

I hope you find these tips helpful when you are trying to get to know someone special. Please feel free to try each of them separately or in combination with each other. Do whatever works to help you forge a strong relationship with your future spouse.

CHAPTER 11: WRAP-UP

Over the years, I have gone to great lengths to meet women. Some of my attempts were successful, and some weren't. Using the methods and tips described above, I have had great times with many different ladies, gaining new perspectives on life and exchanging views on interesting topics. By meeting new women from different backgrounds, I came to understand what was important to me in a relationship. I also learned to express what I wanted, and by stating these desires upfront, I found that my relationships were more honest and fulfilling. When I meet someone new, now my first intention is to get to know her as a person, not to evaluate her as a potential spouse. I am doing all I can to prepare myself for my soulmate whenever—or if ever— God feels I am ready for her.

CHAPTER 11: TAKEAWAYS

DATING

POINTS TO CONSIDER

1. If you write up a list of the attributes you're looking for in a spouse, you can use it to assess a new dating relationship and determine if you want to pursue it further.

2. Nowadays, you have many creative ways to meet someone new, including face-to-face meetings, online dating, and the implementation of various forms of technology. Go ahead and try out a few different methods. The more you use each of them, the better you'll understand what works for you and the more confident you'll become while dating.

3. If you have the opportunity to go on a date, by all means, go and enjoy every minute of it. Let your feelings flow without rushing things. Take your time, and meet in various settings with different people so that you'll get to experience the relationship under a variety of conditions.

QUESTIONS FOR GROUPS

1. What attributes do you value in a person?

2. How do you like to meet new people? What method has worked best for you in the past?

ACTION STEPS TO TAKE

1. Select one of the nine methods listed under the heading "Creative Ways to Meet New People."

2. Try it. See how well it works for you. If unsuccessful, try another method.

CHAPTER 12

THRIVING

From an essential-perspective, you want to have lots of stimulating, stretching, entertaining, and beautiful areas of your life.

—DR. BENJAMIN HARDY, PSYCHOLOGIST AND AUTHOR

STORY OF A SINGLE

I've dated two church guys before, but they weren't the right guys for me. God guided me in those relationships and told me when to shut the door on each of them. I'm glad, because looking back, I see that He protected me.

As a single person, I've experienced God's romantic love for me. He defines me, tells me I'm beautiful, and has built my identity in Him. Whenever I feel rejected by a man, I always remind myself, "God picks me, and I'm beautiful to Him."

I have times when I'm like, "Yeah. Woohoo. Being single is awesome." But then sometimes I worry, like, "Oh dear. Am I not able to commit to a relationship?" Sometimes I feel so lonely and wonder, "What's wrong with me? Am I not skinny enough? Am I not pretty enough?"

Don't let your singleness make you feel less of a human, less awesome, less beautiful, less handsome, or less anything. There's nothing wrong with you just because you are single, and you don't need anyone else to tell you that. I find I don't need validation from another person because my quality of life depends on getting close to God. God will always want to be close to you, and when you're single, you realize that you need it. Even when you're married, you have to hold onto God's closeness. Your lover will never be able to fill your heart fully. God alone will satisfy it.

I have turned down attractive non-Christian guys who had a lot going for them. That was hard for me to do. In those types of moments, I say, "I'm bleeding out some life right now. Give me the Bible." I know that my life depends on the Bible because, in times like those, it gives me the strength I need to keep myself from compromising. God understands everything and He meets my needs. The best gift that God has ever given me is a hunger for Him. And that hunger is the one thing that I would hold onto until the very end of my days because I know if you hunger for God, nothing will be an issue.

Christians love preaching about getting married and bringing fruitfulness to the Kingdom of God as a couple. Scripture says, "Two will put ten thousand to flight," and "a three-stranded cord is not easily broken." As singles, sometimes we feel like our lives aren't as valued. My life has been full of those moments. But on the other hand, I have experienced God using me powerfully to do great things. I'm most proud of the times God used me to impact other people, and I can see their lives changed because of me. Like one friend, who wasn't really into church. I brought her to a Christian camp with me, and now she's a thriving leader in her church community.

The key to success is being humbled by God. When you are humble, He can give you the tools you need to succeed. Meekness of heart is important, too. I live my life being accountable for every minute and second that God gives me, praying that it honors Him every time. I want people to come to my funeral and say, "My life changed because Judith shared her love for Jesus with me." These last thirty-two years have gone pretty quickly. My time here on earth is like a rehearsal before Heaven. I want to work hard during the rehearsal because when performing time comes, I want to focus on God and prepare for eternity. And on that final day, when I come face to face with God, He will see my little beating heart, and I will share in an even greater measure of joy in His presence.

—JUDITH, THIRTY-TWO YEARS OLD, NEW ZEALAND

As a single person, you can choose to thrive. It's within your reach. All you have to do is to decide to start. No matter where you live, no matter how rich you are, and no matter what your educational level is, you can thrive by living your life to its fullest potential. In other words:

To get all there is out of living, we must employ our time wisely, never being in too much of a hurry to stop and sip life, but never losing our sense of the enormous value of a minute.

—ROBERT UPDEGRAFF, AUTHOR AND MANAGEMENT CONSULTANT

Let us focus on making the best use of our single season. Imagine squeezing an orange and getting every single drop of juice out of it. Likewise, our lives are precious. As singles, we have become accustomed to living with less. That is a tragedy because we won't experience thriving if we do not reach to attain it. It is like playing a video game and not realizing there is another bonus level. Sometimes as singles, we do not look to thrive. But we can. And that is what I want for all of us.

International social media influencer and real estate mogul, Grant Cardone, suggests that to reach our full potential, we must choose things we consider to be out of our reach. "Don't just think about what is realistic. The problem with realistic thinking is that it's usually based on what others think is possible. They don't know your potential. Whenever you start a task with a mind toward the potential outcome, you will limit the actions required to accomplish that goal."

Maybe you have a limited view of your potential? And, because of that, you are not thriving? Or maybe you are unsure of what to do to reach your full potential. How exactly can you thrive?

BE GENEROUS

Being a giver is not good for a 100-yard dash, but it's valuable in a marathon.

—ADAM GRANT, PSYCHOLOGIST AND AUTHOR

The happiest people are the ones who give. The long-term wealthy people typically have one thing in common: they are generous. This shows that generosity is an important muscle to build. But to be generous, you do not need money or a car or a house. All you need is time. We each have twenty-four hours every day we can use to do good.

Besides giving a percentage of my income away, I am also committed to being intentional with my time, as well. I deliberately schedule time to do things in service for others with a goal of dedicating at least 10 percent of my time to helping others. For many years, I have served at my local church, and now, I serve as a volunteer in Cambodia. In fact, I currently give away almost all my time. I do have some personal projects, including writing blog articles, writing this book, consulting for pharmaceutical companies, and new projects I am undertaking, but most of my time is taken up with my service to the Cambodian education project.

Psychologist and author Dr. Benjamin Hardy says the successful do not work for money; they work to learn. My motivation in serving here, however, is not money or learning but rather helping to build God's Kingdom. I want to make Jesus's name great. I am so grateful for the opportunity to provide service to the children of Cambodia by giving my time, wisdom, energy, and knowledge. And I am very thankful for all that I have learned while doing so, including a myriad of technical, emotional, and interpersonal skills. I never expected to receive so much in return for my generosity.

The most important gift I've received is the realization that being generous makes me happy. I like to receive things. When I get a present, or if my friend does something nice for me, I rejoice. But when I serve, I feel profound satisfaction I recognize as thriving. Nothing else in the world could make me feel that good and inspire me to work even harder to get more of that as-good-as-it-gets feeling.

Are you curious about generosity and how you can incorporate it into your life? It's simple to do. Just stop living for yourself and start giving your money, time, wisdom, knowledge, skills, encouraging words, smile, comforting hug, and words of affirmation to the people around you who need them. And do not expect anything in return. As Jesus said, "It is more blessed to give than to receive" (Acts 20:35).

I dream of a generation of singles so generous that the world notices us. That's the kind of person I want to marry, too. Our relationship will start at another level because we have this life-transforming habit of giving, which fuels this virtuous cycle of "you first." Let us become a community of the most generous people on the planet.

In addition to encouraging you to freely give your time, I also urge you to become generous in another area: with your money. "What? How personal!" you might say. I'm sure you did not buy this book expecting me to tell you to give away your money. Yet, I have noticed in my life that if I want to thrive, I must give my money, too. Like me, as a single person, I bet you have more of a financial margin than a family with children. Giving money away does something wonderful to your heart and takes your focus away from yourself and your self-centered desires, providing you with a sense of deep satisfaction. Also, by giving money, you can have a significant impact on the lives of others.

CHANGING A NATION THROUGH HIGH-QUALITY EDUCATION

In 2016, being single and receiving a pay raise enabled me to co-initiate an education scholarship program in Cambodia. Instead of increasing my personal spending to take advantage of my raise, I decided to maintain my current lifestyle and bank the additional money. I never imagined that dozens of students would one day get a better education because of this simple decision. But it didn't stop there. I decided to take my generosity to another level by resigning from my career in the biotech industry and moving to Cambodia.

Historically, many Cambodian children drop out of school. Because of this lack of education, they struggle to secure stable employment and thus are at an increased risk of becoming victims of human trafficking and slavery. When I heard about this problem, I thought someone should do something about this lack of education. Then I read this quote by apartheid activist and South African President Nelson Mandela: "Education is the most powerful weapon you can use to change the world." I decided to become someone who did something. What better way to use my time, talent, and treasure to affect a change? The more I looked into the education problem in Cambodia, the larger my project grew in scope.

I now have big dreams for our program. Access to excellent education will change the lives of hundreds of thousands of young Cambodians for the better. Their future will be much brighter because they will be given the tools to craft them for themselves. To accomplish this, our team will assist an increasing number of students, beginning in the region of Siem Reap. Once we have developed an effective educational system there, my dream is to replicate that model at various locations throughout the country. Starting with the twenty-eight students in our pilot program, we plan to expand to include young people throughout Cambodia.

In embracing this path, I certainly chose the road less-traveled by letting go of my modern comforts, saying "no" to my career, and embracing an uncertain but very exciting future. And yet, amidst all this uncertainty, I thrive, crazy enough to believe I can change the world. Steve Jobs said:

Here's to the crazy ones. The misfits. The rebels. The troublemakers. The round pegs in the square holes. The ones who see things differently. They're not fond of rules. And they have no respect for the status quo. You can quote them, disagree with them, glorify or vilify them. About the only thing you can't do is ignore them. Because they change things. They push the human race forward. And while some may see them as the crazy ones, we see genius. Because the people who are crazy enough to think they can change the world, are the ones who do.

You, too, have the opportunity to become a strategic influencer of your world. God blesses you with money, talents, time, knowledge, and wisdom. How are you going to use these valuable tools to make a difference?

We make a living by what we get. We make a life by what we give.

—WINSTON S. CHURCHILL, STATESMAN AND WRITER

Give, but give until it hurts.

—MOTHER TERESA, NUN AND MISSIONARY

YOU HOLD THE KEYS IN YOUR HAND

You have the power to make your current season the most meaningful one you have ever experienced. All you have to do is to decide to shift gears and take the on-ramp up to the interstate of your future. You are one decision away from becoming the most passionate person in your environment. Really!

I used to see myself as a victim rather than a conqueror. Somewhere in my childhood, I lost my sense of heroism. But then, when I chose generosity and passion, everything changed for me. I believe now is the time for me to live to the fullest. As Jesus says:

> *I have come that they may have life, and have it to the full.*
>
> **—JOHN 10:10 (NIV)**

You can decide to start living and leave behind the self-doubt, frustration, and depression caused by your singleness. You can make it happen. As we have seen before, we cannot influence when we are going to meet Mr. Betterhalf or Miss Princess. And at the end of the day, that doesn't matter. If we learn to become complete in Jesus, we can thrive at any moment of our lives. Don't waste a minute more; decide now to become a single influencer.

LEAVING A LEGACY

We have covered much ground in this book. You and I no longer look at what is lacking in our lives, we have worked on our past to prepare ourselves for our futures, and we understand that great things are in store for us. But how do you want others to remember you after your time here on earth is over? What do you want to leave behind as your legacy?

To start preparing your legacy, let me encourage you to live your best life now. Use your tools to make a difference. A big dream often starts small, with a dream in our heart that swells and grows, like the Bible's mustard seed that becomes a large tree in the end. To make your dream into your legacy, start small, and then allow it to steadily build. Leadership expert, author, and pastor John C. Maxwell wrote, "It takes time for little things to add up to big things. So be consistent." He discovered the compounding power of consistency:

Right choices + Consistency + Time
= Significant Returns

Dr. Maxwell is now in his seventies and has experienced the power of compounding in his life. He made it his mission to train new leaders who, in turn, will train other leaders. Similarly, Paul looked to compound his teachings in this letter he sent to his friend Timothy:

The things you have heard me say in the presence of many witnesses entrust to reliable people who will also be qualified to teach others.

—2 TIMOTHY 2:2 (NIV)

You are someone who can change the world. But do you want to see a more significant result by compounding your efforts to make even more of a difference? To do this, consider helping others to become purposeful, thriving singles who then can join in the efforts.

THRIVE BY PROVIDING SERVICE TO OTHERS

When we stop living for ourselves, we start thriving. Let us become singles who give our lives to support other people to become better. Research shows what the Bible has revealed to us for many thousands of years: helping others makes you happy. The greatest act of humanity is to live following Jesus's example, which means being generous:

For God so loved the world, that he gave his only Son, that whoever believes in him should not perish but have eternal life.

—JOHN 3:16

When you serve, you will experience a degree of satisfaction you cannot get in any other way. No dopamine kick, trip, hack, or whatever crazy whirl of activities you may imagine can give you such fulfillment. John C. Maxwell says that every single day he strives to find a way to add value to people. That is, he serves others.

Providing service to others can be as small as opening a door for someone. When I was a marketplace manager, this was my favorite way of serving others: I held the door for anyone I could on my way to the cafeteria. One day, as I went to get a coffee, I opened the door for a colleague and said, "Good morning, Steve, how are you?"

"Hi, David. Is there something you wanted from me?" he asked.

"Nope. I just wanted to wish you a great start in the new week."

That made his day, and it made mine, too. I felt happy all day due to this little act of service even though it did not require much effort at all.

God invites you to work alongside Him. Are you ready to make a difference? There are so many who need our help. Below, I've provided a list of just a few possible recipients of our service. Remember, by helping them thrive, we thrive ourselves.

Service #1: To Those in Need

The Bible encourages us to serve others by praying to God and asking Him who we should help. There are so many we could serve for Him. Wherever you look, you'll see people who need what you can offer. The list is endless. It may be people who are without vision, depressed, hungry, alone, jobless, sick, or as in my case, children who lack high-quality education. It's one thing to be kind to people. It's another story to help people truly in need.

When I played in a worship band, a particular song resonated with me: "Solution" by Hillsong United. The song urged us to pray to God to fill our hearts with His compassion and to let us be His hands and feet so that God can work through us. As the song says, He dreams to "mend the broken heart, cause the blind to see, erase complete the sinner's past, set the captives free, take the widow's cry, cause her heart to sin, be a Father to the fatherless." If you and I go all in, "we will be His light on the darkest place."

Service #2: To Society

Have you felt a longing to start a business, write a new worship song, or, like Martin Luther King, Jr. and Mahatma Gandhi, change an entire nation? In your single season, you probably have the time, energy, and money to make your dream a reality and to help society in the process.

There are countless possibilities to use your unique gifts to benefit society. I have helped people in the business world by providing them with high-quality work and a positive attitude. I have often invested time and energy to volunteer at my local church, too. You might consider making a difference in arts and entertainment. Or, perhaps you'll get involved in politics. You may also decide to invest in education in your community or abroad, as I have. Where do you feel God is calling you to take your involvement to another level?

God's invitation to advance His Kingdom comes in other forms, too. Sometimes He asks you to take more responsibility. Perhaps He wants you to work part-time and accept a pay cut, take a sabbatical, or leave your job entirely, so you have time available to do His work. Maybe God wants you to start a new company, something dedicated to helping an under-served segment of society. No matter what God asks you to do, if you obey His calling, you will leave an eternal legacy.

Service #3: To Other Singles

You are one of many amazing singles. When it comes to investing in others, I invite you to look around to see how you could help other singles in your area. Can you assist other singles in your church?

Perhaps you know someone like my friend, Grace, who tried to find her place in her church and made me wonder, "What can I do to help her find a way to become a part of her community as a single?" Since I lived a distance from her, my degree of action was limited. Hence, I became her encourager. That is how I chose to invest in her and help her thrive.

As a community pastor at my church, I did as much as I could to help singles feel welcomed. I wanted to create a safe space for all of us where we could meet and have a good time. One Easter, I suggested we singles gather at my friend Tim's apartment to share an Easter meal, a feast typically shared with family members. That day, we made up our own family, filling Tim's loft with joy. About twenty of us gathered to share what was supposed to be just a meal that became hours of fun community time together. We enjoyed a traditional Easter meal accompanied by tasty wine and then finished it off with cake and ice cream. I felt as if we were part of the early church community described in Acts 2:

*And they devoted themselves to the apostles'
teaching and the fellowship, to the breaking of
bread and the prayers.*

—ACTS 2:42

We worshiped, prayed, and discussed topics important to all of us. And then we watched a movie together because we did not want to go home. "Wow," I thought, "to invest in other singles is so powerful!" Each of us was making the other members of the group feel valued, accepted, and important. In short, we were helping each other thrive.

How can you invest in other singles? I dream about creating a singles community where we support each other and help everyone find creative ideas to serve the singles around us. They need to hear this message of hope: nothing is wrong with you just because you are single. Let us team up to make the single world a better place. I would love to hear your ideas. Please email me at david@singleforaseason.com so that I may share them on my blog. Together, we can make a difference.

Service #4: To Your Pastor

You cannot blame your pastor for not having a vision for singles, especially if he got married in his twenties. The increasing number of singles in churches is a new phenomenon, so chances are he never heard about it when he was in seminary. In the church where I serve now, the pastors and the board members have all been married for many years, and they all married young. How can they possibly understand what you and I are going through?

You can help your pastor gain a vision for singles in your church community. I suggest you share this book with him or her and propose leading a singles group there. And why not consider starting an online singles group for multiple campuses or with other churches? You and your pastor can use the questions and material I provide at the end of each chapter to do so. You will see that by sharing these resources, you will help multiple people thrive: your pastor, other singles in your church community, and yourself. Good job!

Service #5: To Your Married Friends

With your married friends, your service to them may take the form of helping them comprehend what it's like to be a single person and thus understand you better. To do this, you can share the testimonials of the singles I have interviewed in this book. Perhaps they will show your married friends that there is nothing wrong with you because you are single and that your singleness does not mean you have unreasonable expectations or fear relationships.

When I celebrated my fortieth birthday, I threw a party and had a lot of fun. I didn't feel like a forty-year-old at all. But I did sense a degree of unease in my married friends there, because of my relationship status. At the time, I remember thinking that I wished they understood the single experience better.

Perhaps, you too, wish to be understood. Wouldn't it be great if your married friends would cheer you on instead of contributing to you feeling inadequate because of your values and choices? They may fear that you're missing out. Or perhaps they are not feeling comfortable because they made different choices. Maybe they don't understand the value of your single season.

If singles like us showed married couples a way for us to team up with them, great things would happen. I believe God wants this. I think He wants marrieds and singles to work together. Each group is capable of doing things the other cannot. Our unique life experiences, perspectives, roles, and responsibilities make us complementary so that together, we could more than double our efforts and results. In other words, one plus one would equal more than two. If single and married people work together, we can maximize this potential and accomplish great things.

A big part of thriving is figuring out how you can assist those who don't understand you yet, or help the people who have a different perspective than yours. Despite disagreements, we can move forward hand in hand. As an example of this, look at the political system in Switzerland. In the Federal Council—our executive branch—seven ministers from four different political parties must cooperate. In this one group, we have both left-wing and right-wing members. Their power comes from their capability and willingness to find a consensus, often referred to as the Helvetic Compromise. The Federal Council is a key element of the Swiss success story. For more than 150 years, we have managed to navigate through complicated matters because we respect opposing opinions and try to find a common denominator.

Likewise, such cooperation between us singles, who have more time and resources available, and married people, who are often more grounded and have a somewhat more comprehensive perspective, fires me up. To quote the motto of Manchester United, an exceptional United Kingdom soccer team, "United we stand." You and I can make it happen because we know what a long-term single life looks like and how we can leverage it to leave a legacy. I encourage you to share this book with your married friends. Increased awareness may prompt them to encourage us in our single season. If they know what challenges singles face, they can pray for us, invite us over for a cup of tea, or send us a message saying, "Well done! Keep it up!" And if they develop the same vision of cooperation as we do, they will be able to recognize the potential that lies in us teaming up. Your married friends may have no idea that you can thrive as a single person. Show them that you are part of a great singles community and are living a fulfilled life and thriving.

No matter to whom you decide to dedicate your service—those in need, your society, other singles, your pastor, or married people—know that this service is performed in God's name, and by this service, you will help others thrive and you will thrive yourself.

YOU CAN DO IT!

And now let me talk to you about doubt. If you are like me, you may wonder how you can make a difference. You may think, "Sure. Others are crushing it—changing the world for the better. But they know the right people, have a lot of money, and have thousands of ideas. What tools do I have to work with?"

Let me say this to you: "If you believe in God, you have all you need." Look at what Paul said to the Philippians:

I can do all things through him who
strengthens me.

—PHILIPPIANS 4:13

Do not forget that if you are a follower of Christ, you can do all things through Him. You don't have to rely on your know-how and energy alone. Jesus will give you courage, strength, and willpower to keep going when you face roadblocks. He'll provide joy in the middle of challenges and the right connections at the right moment. He will lead you to places of influence you would not have imagined. Doors you could not possibly open yourself will suddenly be opened for you by His grace.

CHAPTER 12: WRAP-UP

You deserve a life that is rich with beautiful experiences. And you should thrive at your fullest potential now and when you meet your soulmate. Leadership coach Robin Sharma wrote, "Nothing will fill your heart with a greater sense of regret than lying on your deathbed knowing that you did not live your life and do your dreams." What a pity it would be if you missed out on this extraordinary opportunity you have in your single season. If we manage to detach ourselves from our concerns about our relationship status and start thriving, we will live our lives to their fullest.

In the Book of Acts, when Paul departed from Ephesus to go back to Jerusalem, his friends tried to dissuade him from doing so, knowing he might get arrested. But Paul was focused on doing one thing: accomplishing his mission for God:

You yourselves know how I lived among you the whole time from the first day that I set foot in Asia, serving the Lord with all humility and with tears and with trials that happened to me through the plots of the Jews; how I did not shrink from declaring to you anything that was profitable, and teaching you in public and from house to house, testifying both to Jews and to Greeks of repentance toward God

and of faith in our Lord Jesus Christ. And now,
behold, I am going to Jerusalem, constrained by
the Spirit, not knowing what will happen to me
there, except that the Holy Spirit testifies to me
in every city that imprisonment and afflictions
await me. But I do not account my life of any
value nor as precious to myself, if only I may
finish my course and the ministry that I received
from the Lord Jesus, to testify to the gospel of
the grace of God.

—ACTS 20:18-24

Paul was thriving, and it was impossible to stop his momentum. He told his friends, "I want to give everything so that I leave a legacy. My purpose is to announce the good news of Jesus Christ. I live to build God's Kingdom." My wish is that we follow Paul's example by becoming people who fulfill the ministry Jesus gave us to do. That is why we are here on planet Earth. Our current relationship status is unimportant. Let us thrive as singles, and when we do get married, keep pressing on toward the goal to receive the heavenly prize for which God is calling us. Let us thrive at every moment of our lives.

And now, go and change the world around you. You know your promised land is waiting for you—a land of astonishment and abundance. You are not alone. Others will join you on this journey. May God's favor be upon you and a thousand generations.

To conclude, I offer you this prayer in the form of promises God made to his people, the Israelites, in Numbers 6:24-26 (NIV), Deuteronomy 31:8 (NIV), and Ezekiel 36:9 & 11:

The Lord bless you
and keep you;
the Lord make his face shine on you
and be gracious to you;
the Lord turn his face toward you
and give you peace.
The Lord himself goes before you
and will be with you;
he will never leave you nor forsake you.

Do not be afraid;
do not be discouraged.

I am for you,
and I will turn to you,
and will do more good to you than ever before.

Amen

CHAPTER 12: TAKEAWAYS
THRIVING

POINTS TO CONSIDER

1.   To thrive, you must first become a generous person. The happiest people are the ones who give money, share their knowledge, and offer their time to others.

2.   You can make your single season the most meaningful one you have ever experienced.

3.   In your single season, you have a wonderful opportunity to help other people have better lives. This is a once-in-a-lifetime opportunity for you to leverage your resources and to change your world. Start small and then make your dream into your legacy.

QUESTIONS FOR GROUPS

1.   What changes do you need to make in your life to start thriving as a single?

2.   How can you use your money, talents, time, knowledge, and wisdom to change your world?

3.   What stops you from living your legacy? How can you overcome these obstacles?

ACTION STEPS TO TAKE

1. In your journal, write down your world-changing dream: a specific way you would like to serve others.

2. Write up a list of steps you can take—one each day—to achieve this dream.

3. Do step #1. Then tomorrow, do step #2. Continue until your dream is achieved.

NEXT STEPS

Are you ready to take the next steps and deepen into the ideas in this book?

Please visit **www.singleforaseason.com** to learn more about additional resources helping you to live fulfilled in your single season including:

Group workbook—how to thrive in your singleness

•

Inspirational blog articles

•

Online workshops

FREE BONUS

Get your FREE copy of The Seven Habits of Remarkably Happy Singles

www.singleforaseason.com/bonus

ACKNOWLEDGMENTS

For me, writing this book has been much like reaching the top of a tall mountain, one I initially thought would be impossible to climb. The process has been much more challenging than I anticipated and more rewarding than I could have ever dreamed. Many people helped me made this seemingly impossible dream a reality, and I would like to take this opportunity to thank them from the bottom of my heart.

I owe an immense debt of gratitude to those singles and used-to-be-long-term-singles who allowed themselves to become vulnerable by sharing their stories: Matt, Olivier, Stephanie, Phil, Chrystel, Sopheap, Annie, Véronique, Laurent, Ruth, Céline, and Judith. Your unique experiences powerfully enrich the book and make it much more impactful by providing a wide variety of relatable perspectives.

I'm also grateful for my cheerleaders who kept me going throughout the project, particularly my friends: Phil, Ben, Kevin, Juliette, Judith, and Claire. Your thumbs-ups, cheers, words of encouragement, and frequent questions about my progress helped me stay the course. Sarah, Marjory, and Mukti, thank you for your critique of the first draft of the manuscript that provided valuable feedback and helped me refine my message. And thanks to all who prayed for me. Your prayers helped the fountain of great ideas flow whenever I engaged in yet another writing session.

I extend a special thank-you to my parents, Ingrid and Karl, who believed in this project from the very beginning. It's such an honor to have you at my side. And thank you for reminding me to put the book out in the world, keeping the deadline in mind.

Micha, Christina, and Elia; and Raphael and Martina, my dear brothers and their families, thank you for the quality time you have shared with me. I love you all.

The right environment was vital for me to craft this book. Thank you, Lisa Tener (LisaTener.com), for providing a well-designed book-writing course that gave us participants the tools to write our first drafts in less than three months. Joshua, thank you for telling me, "The world needs your book." And thank you, Sagara, for the weekly accountability calls. I still remember your comment about my book vision paragraph: "By reading this, I can tell this book is definitely going to happen." And thanks to all other course participants for your valuable advice.

To my many mentors whose books, articles, and videos helped me understand that even the best writers suffer from writer's block, I offer this note of gratitude. Your words of wisdom also gave me the permission I needed to write the necessary ugly first draft.

Thank you, Lynne Heinzmann (LynneHeinzmann.com), for being my invaluable editor. You performed editorial magic, making the manuscript so much better while keeping my voice.

Thanks also to Howard VanEs (LetsWriteBooks.net) and his team for their book design, proofreading, and marketing expertise, and for overseeing all of all the details of the self-publishing process. Claire Francis, thank you for your careful review of the manuscript. Your attention to detail allowed you to identify many important little things to fix.

I extend a special thanks to all my sponsors. As a church and NGO volunteer living in Cambodia, I had limited resources. Your financial contributions enabled me to greatly increase the impact of *Single for a Season* by investing in high-quality editing and marketing.

Finally, thank you to pastor Chris Hodges, who prompted me and the other participants of the Hillsong Europe conference in London to write a bucket list. You encouraged me to dream big, which inspired me to write this book.

ABOUT THE AUTHOR

David Brühlmann's dream of getting married and having a family has not yet become a reality. Instead, he has decided to help singles make the most out of their single season. Currently he runs online meetups, discussion groups, webinars, workshops, and writes inspiring blog articles on Medium, encouraging singles to be happy and perhaps help change the world. David is also in the process of creating and building a multi-media, multi-faceted resource website for singles.

David has also been an innovative scientist holding an MSc. in chemical engineering and a Ph.D. in biology and is known for excellent articles in peer-reviewed journals and entertaining talks at biotechnology conferences. Having understood how to leverage the advantage of singleness, in 2019, David renounced his corporate carrier to dedicate his life to the development of high-quality education for children and young adults in Cambodia.

In his free time, David travels the world, enjoys outdoor sports, plays the piano, and empowers others in his local church.

CONNECT WITH DAVID HERE:

🏠 singleforaseason.com

📷 instagram.com/davebruehlmann

f facebook.com/people/David-Br%C3%BChmann/808120240

in linkedin.com/in/david-br%C3%BChlmann-134960b